The Perfect Imperfect Wife

THE PERFECT IMPERFƏCT WIFE

Published by
CONSTANT MEDIA GROUP™
P.O. Box 26806
Scottsdale, AZ 85255
Constant Media Group™ is a registered trademark of Constant Media Group™

Editorial Director, Elizabeth Rattray

New paperback edition published 2021
ISBN 978-0-9985065-6-2
Printed in the United States of America

The Library of Congress Cataloging-in-Publications Data
Constant, D. C. The Perfect Imperfect Wife, My Journey in To Wifehood

Unless otherwise stated, all Scriptural quotations are taken from the Holy Bible King James Version, New Living Translation (NLT), New International Version (NIV), The Message Bible (MSG), New International Reader's Version (NIRV), New Life Version (NLV), and Good News Translation (GNT).

The internet addresses, email addresses, and phone numbers in this book are accurate at the time of publication. They are provided as a resource.

Note: This publication contains the opinions and ideas of its author. It is intended to provide helpful and informative matériel on the subject matter. It is sold with the understanding that the author and publisher are not engaged in rendering professional services in this book. If the reader requires personal assistance or advice, a competent licensed professional should be consulted. The author and publisher specifically disclaim responsibility for any liability, loss, or risk, personal or otherwise, which is incurred as a consequence, directly or indirectly, of the use and application of any of the contents of this book

My Journey into Wifehood

The Perfect Imperfect Wife

D.C. Constant

DEDICATION

To My Superman of a husband,
D. Lee Constant

You're not only my Best Friend, Lover and Pastor, but you're truly a Man of God and a Man of Faith.

Thank you for loving me how Jesus Christ loves the church... Unconditionally. You have loved and continue to love me with a "No Strings Attached Love," which is scarce, extremely rare, which most people, yet alone a wife, ever experience during their lifetime.

I'm truly humbled and it has been my honor and a pleasure being your wife for the past 25 years and the years to come! The love you give and express to me, is the closet image I have to understanding God's unconditional love towards me.

Infinity ~ Dar Dar

"There isn't any 'big secret' to having a lasting healthy marriage, but there will be a need to have a 'big heart' filled with forgivenessand unconditional love, to overcome the multitude of faults you both will have."

D.C. CONSTANT

CONTENTS

OTHER BOOKS

by D.C. CONSTANT

It Might Just Be You!

Stacking The Deck Series:

The Race Card, The Church Card,
The Office Card, and The Family Card

Don't Talk! Just Do The Work!

(Exclusively on Author's Website)
www.dcconstant.com

In Memoriam

Grandma Bernice Gresham

Grandma Mary Alice Underwood

My Beloved June Rose Cox

ACKNOWLEDGEMENTS

Thanking God for just being God and for joining together what no man can put asunder. ~Mark 10:9

To my wonderful editor, Elizabeth "Liz" Rattray. Liz, you deliver with excellence time and time again! For the past 30 years, I've valued both our professional and personal friendship. You're truly loved and appreciated more than you will ever know!

To my business partner Jon-Michael Thomas. Thank you for your friendship and support throughout the years. I appreciate you, your heart, integrity, authenticity and the kindness you've always shown to me and my husband. We love you and your family dearly!

To Sean A. Cox Sr. and Cynthia Cox-Lessears. The love I have for you both is immeasurable. You have absolutely no idea how the both of you were 'life savers' during a trying time in my life. We are family, bonded for life. I love you both. *Always Familia.*

FOREWORD

By: Jon-Michael Thomas

Today we live in a world where the concept, idea, definition and necessity of marriage has been questioned often and greatly disputed. Postmodernism has caused many, even professed Bible- believing Christians, to refrain from taking any solid stance on the importance of marriage, the purpose of marriage, or the rules by which couples should govern their marriage.

With so many pervasive opinions and interpretations of marriage it is no wonder many couples find themselves confused about what they believe and what marriage should look like; as they are unsettled on the benefits and even the blessings of marriage. Many have never seen a godly marriage modeled in front of them. Couple that with trying to reconcile what the Bible says about marriage juxtaposed to one's own upbringing and lived experiences, you then have a situation that easily transforms confusion to fear.

Both men and women struggle with fears when it comes to marriage, but for many women fear is not the main issue. The main issue is security. It is a well-known statistic that 25% of women in America have been sexually abused (usually a trusted relative, family friend, or someone close to them). In addition to sexual abuse, 33% of women in America have been physically abused by someone close to them. And over 48% of women in America have been emotionally abused by someone close to them. What do these numbers mean?

They mean abuse is the only thing many women have ever known. They mean many women may find it difficult to feel secure if they decide to accept a marriage proposal. They mean that even after marriage many women will need to work through a lot of issues to become emotionally healthy enough to contribute or participate within a healthy marriage relationship. Sadly, many never receive the tools needed to recover from all the trauma they have experienced and operate within the confines of a healthy marriage that can be emulated by their children. Cycles. Generational cycles. Hard to break cycles often ensue.

This book, *The Perfect Imperfect Wife*, needed to be written in order to provide triage to trauma and to provide the tools to break the torment of these generational cycles. Without reservation, I wholeheartedly believe that D.C. Constant is ordained by God to be a woman anointed for such at time as this; breaking chains of insecurity and destroying the heavy burdensome yokes of Satan, which have held many captives.

Constant's transparency is on full display as she takes us through her past and her personal journey. Though extremely relatable, she never portrays herself as a victim. Her vulnerability is on exhibit as she details her circumstances and coming of age, but she never uses her abuse as an excuse or license to abuse drugs, alcohol or promiscuity; the usual self-prescriptions many have used to anesthetize their pain. Violations of her trust by those who should have been there to father her and protect her did not cause her to hate men or hate God. Although she had every reason to abandon hope in love, marriage and men, she never lost her faith in God or His plans for her life. And God rewarded her unwavering faith with real love, a great husband, a strong marriage, a divine calling and an awesome testimony.

This book is full of wisdom, helpful tools, an example that will resonate with you as you read. And I promise, if you read this book with an open heart and take heed to the lessons taught, you too will find yourself with an awesome testimony of your own and every ungodly cycle broken. A final word: Always remember that God is the Master of transforming all of our imperfections and broken pieces into a perfect masterpiece!

Selah.

INTRODUCTION

The making of a wife starts long before her walk down the aisle, from her carefully chosen beautiful gown, to her handsome groom, as he waits to join and take her hand in holy matrimony as they utter those two magical words, "I Do."

It starts when she's a young, impressionable little girl, listening to fairytales, often read to her before bedtime. You know, the fairytales where the princess is portrayed as a damsel in distress, and her knight and shining armor the prince comes and save the day? The Prince was 'PERFECT' and they both lived happily ever after.

In real life, the perspective on marriage and what it means to be a wife will vary. The factors will include religion, era, family traditions, demographics, regions, and economic status. They can range from traditional marriage to contemporary and everything in between.

I grew up in a much more traditional era, were society already had perceived roles for husbands and wives. The husband was considered the only 'ruler,' 'breadwinner,' and 'defender,' of the home. The wife's role was 'homemaker,' and 'mother.' If she was lucky to work outside of the home, she could be a 'teacher' or a 'nurse.'

While I do not find anything wrong with these traditional roles, it appeared to limit wives to stereotypical professions, without encouragement to work outside of the home, given inspiration to aspire in other professions, or even offering a choice to do both.

In the following chapters, we will explore specific areas in my life, which set the course for my journey into wifehood. I trust you will enjoy my few tidbits of wisdom, sprinkled with a touch of witty sarcasm.

This book is for the wife who understands she isn't "Perfect," but she's 'PERFECTLY IMPERFECT' just for her husband. You recognize your both God's gift to one another and you desire to do what's pleasing and honorable in the sight of God.

Wives, please understand this book isn't a guide for "How to Be A Better Wife" or "How to 'Be A Wife" like D.C. CONSTANT, as it would be an impossible task, because well... you're not me, and you're not married to my husband.

You are a wife God designed with purpose, uniquely embodied with her own authenticity and beauty for your husband.

As you read through the book, catching a glimpse of my life, my prayer is you see and appreciate my heart's journey, having a renewed perspective of hope and redemption for your own personal wifehood journey.

I want you to know, it didn't take me twenty-five years to learn the lessons from my marriage, that I'm choosing to share now.

It just took me twenty-five years to decide, it's now the 'Perfect' time to tell you how I became "The Perfect Imperfəct Wife™"

Part One

Understanding My Foundation

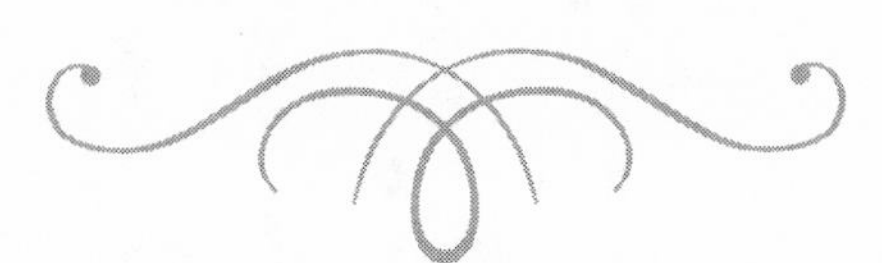

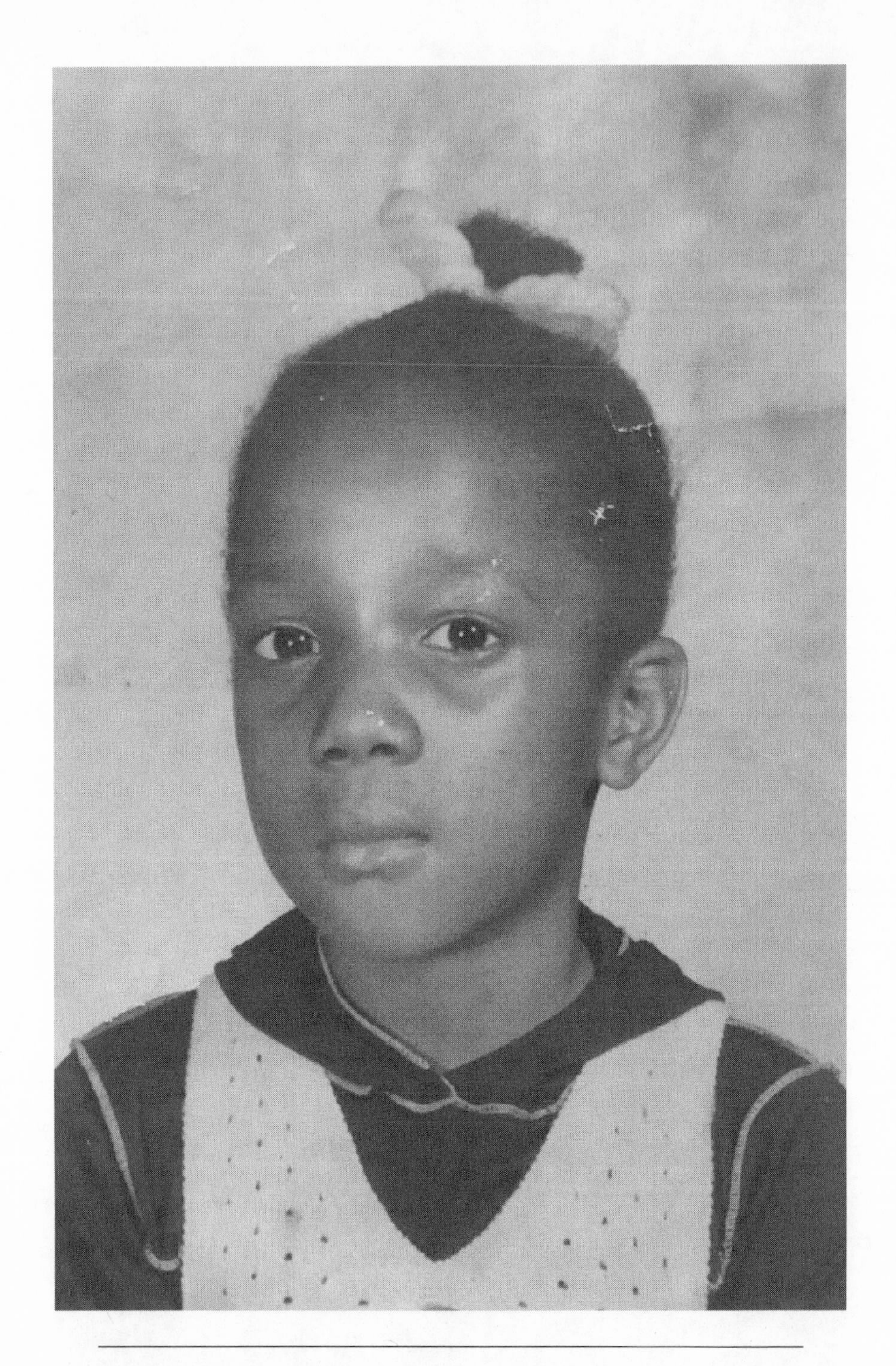

Me: Darlene Gresham at 6 years old

My Genesis

To understand my journey into wifehood, you need to first understand my foundation. Every one of us has a genesis.

A beginning.

A story which starts with a blank canvas, when we're born, entrusted into the care of our parents whom would love, care and protect us from the evil wiles of the world. For some of us, we would soon find ourselves needing protection from them.

Here's a glimpse into my genesis.

My mother was eighteen when I was born, and two years later, she had my sister. Growing up, my mom, sister and I lived in the public housing projects. She was a single mother, working as a nurse's aid. My sister was in daycare, and I was a "latch key" kid. That's when a child came home from school to an empty house, because their parent(s) were still at work.

I was a child with great creativity and a love for reading and writing, which was my "Happy Place." This all changed when at six-years old I was introduce to my stepfather. It wasn't a good introduction.

I was used to my mom having male company over, but they always left. For some reason, this man hadn't left like all the others. He was always in our house.

Me: One day, I whisper to my mom, "When is that man leaving?"

Mom: "Darlene, he's not leaving."

Me: "Why?"

Mom: "He's your new daddy."

Me: "But he ain't my daddy."

Mom: "I'm married now. He's my husband."

I didn't understand what that meant. What's a husband?

Finally, one day my mother called me and my sister into the living room and said, "This is Charles, ya'll new daddy." He looked evil. He was tall, with an afro, and had a mean demeanor.

I just stared at him. My mom kept trying to get us to call him daddy, and I kept shaking my head no. He looked at us and said, "I'm ya'll got damn daddy now, so call me Daddy." I kept shaking my head no. What came out my mouth was "Charlie," and there it was. That's what we called him.

I never called that man Daddy.

From the time my mother and stepfather married, he always called me stupid, as if it were my given birthname. He rarely ever called me Darlene. He told me all the time I was ugly like he was giving me a compliment, and would emphasize how no man would ever want me.

I was six-years old.

This psychological warfare went on every day, continuing through high school. The verbal abuse had become so egregious that for years, I stopped looking at myself in the mirror.

The physical abuse was even as worse.

During my adolescent years, in school, I would always receive good grades, but bad marks for my behavior. My teachers would send notes home stating I was "acting out" in class, being angry and acting like the "class clown." When I got home my mother would read the note, begin screaming, asking me, "Darlene what the hell is wrong with you! You're so fucking retarded with your bad ass! You're just seeking attention?" She would then whoop me and when my stepfather came home I would get another beating.

I was never 'disciplined.' I was beaten. My stepfather, would make me strip naked, and use an extension cord to beat me. I remember begging him not to beat me, saying "Please Charlie, I love you, please, please, please stop." I didn't love him, but I wanted him to stop beating on my fragile black body and so I said, what I felt would get him to stop. It didn't work. He continued beating on my black tiny body anyway.

I can still see all the extension cords around the house. There was the brown one, the black one and a red & silver colored one. The red & silver colored one hurt the most, because it was the thickest of all the extension cords.

As a child, it never mattered what I had done. If I was good, I was still told I was a 'bad ass child.' If I messed up, I was still a "bad ass child."

I had begun acting out even more in school with my behavior and I started wetting the bed, something I had never done before. I wet the bed well into my early pre-teens. My mom didn't make the connection with my wetting the bed due to the abuse. She just called me a "piss pot," and my bed wetting became the butt of family jokes.

Unlike phone hot lines today where children can call someone, or go to a program and speak about their feelings, etc... I had no one to talk to. The era I grew up in, children were to be seen, not heard and you definitely did not talk to anyone outside the home about what was taking place on the inside.

My teachers were all perplexed about the same thing. My school work was excellent, but they could not understand the sudden change in my behavior.

What I could not express at the age of six years old was, the sudden changes in my behavior were due to the abuse taking place at home. My home life was very confusing for me. I went from having a home with only my mother and sister to having a strange man living with us. I was now being verbally and physically abused. The atmosphere in our home had changed to the point I had begun to have anxiety and was on edge all the time. I also had to watch my mother get physical and verbally abused as well.

How does a six-year-old cope in that atmosphere?

No one ever asked, "The Why Question."

"Why had Darlene's behavior changed?"

I was reduced to being called and known as "Bad Ass Darlene" not only from the school teachers, but family members began calling me this as well.

Perhaps my mother didn't protect me, because she was busy dodging blows herself. Watching my stepfather beat my mother, shaped how I viewed marriage and what it meant to be a wife.

I knew by the age of six-years old; I didn't want to be anyone's wife.

The picture of the "Perfect Marriage" in my mind looked something like this: I would grow up, get married, have a baby, get divorced, and raise the child alone. It would just be me and my baby and no husband or father in the picture. The only reason I would get married is so the child wouldn't be born out-of-wedlock and labeled a bastard.

Crazy thinking right?

I came to this conclusion after watching my stepfather attack my mother. I thought to myself, no 'husband' was going to beat me and my child.

One of my earliest memories of watching my mother being physically abused, remains vivid in my mind as if it happened yesterday. I'm not sure what set my stepfather off this particular time.

> *"Domestic violence is any behavior involving physical, psychological, emotional, sexual or verbal abuse"*
> **~AUTHOR ASA DON BROWN**

I remember standing in the kitchen. As a child, it looked much bigger than it actually was. It was probably no more than 70sq feet. It had an old white gas stove, white refrigerator, sink and a little table with two chairs. I remember the white table, because I had sat there plenty of nights, being punished for not eating my food.

My stepfather would make me sit there for hours and say to me, "Darlene you ain't nobody special, you gone eat and not waste this damn food! If you got to sit here all damn night, you will."

I was a picky eater, so my mom would fix me my favorite foods to ensure I would eat and not go hungry. He put a stop to her cooking me a different meal, so I would fall asleep many nights sitting at that table.

I'm still a picky eater.

There I stood in the kitchen. Hearing screaming, cursing and yelling, but didn't see anyone. Then I saw my mom crawling on her hands and knees making her way into the little walk-way which led into the kitchen. The floor was made of brown fake wood and there was a black trash can placed up against the wall.

My mom was screaming because her husband was beating her with the strap he used when walking his dogs. She was screaming JESUS, JESUS, JESUS, JESUS JEEEEEUSSS while lying on the floor blocking his blows.

"Please Charles stop," she begged him. She was crying hard.

He kept beating her.

As I stood there watching, I remember having this thought, "Jesus, whoever you are, why won't you save my mommy? She's calling for you."

While getting up, she was still crying and screaming as she walked toward their bedroom. My stepfather then picked up an ash tray and threw it with such force, it struck her in the back, causing a deep gash with blood gushing everywhere. Even, after all these years, she still has the deep-rooted scars on her back. I can still hear and will never forget her screams.

You know, some of the most "educated" people with all their degrees are always saying, "Children are resilient" or "Children won't remember their trauma." Let me say this: The lie detector determined: That's a LIE.

It isn't "resilience." It's suppressed trauma!

The effects of trauma may not be seen immediately in some children, but please understand this: Trauma experienced and carried by children will remain suppressed until it's dealt with in a healthy environment for healing. If the trauma goes unchecked, it will manifest itself in one way another.

The effects of my abuse and trauma would become my '*normal*' well into my teen years and would have an impact into my early adulthood. (*Which will discuss in later chapters.*)

You may be wondering, "Where was my biological father?

Dead.

He had survived serving in the Vietnam war, only to die in a horrific car accident, while on leave for a home visit, with my mom and his family.

I did attend his funeral. My mom was four months pregnant with me when he died. He was 19 years old.

Before his untimely demise, they were engaged and he knew my mom was preggo and was looking forward to meeting me and having lots of kids with my mom.

The Merry-Go-Round

As the years pass, my stepfather's verbal, physical and emotional abuse increased and in between those years my mother would find the courage to leave him, only to go back. This ring around the not so "rosy" merry-go-round went on for years.

She would leave. He would beg, plead, cry, buy flowers, make tons of hollow promises, buy something new for my sister and I, take us to fun places, etc., only for things to fall back into dysfunction within two-weeks. It was always an illusion with him, making promises to not abuse her anymore.

I remember when I thought my mom was done with him for good. She had found a one-bedroom apartment for herself, my sister and I. The apartment was empty, we had no furniture, limited food in the refrigerator and a box spring (*no mattress*) to sleep on, which was placed in the middle of the living room floor.

Can I tell you what I felt?

HAPPINESS!!!

I was so elated with the quietness. It was quiet and peaceful. I didn't care how hard that box spring was or how we didn't have enough food in the fridge, because my mom made sure we ate every day.

I was in "Heaven!"

Then Hell came knocking again, as living on our own was short lived. For whatever reason, my mom announced we were moving back to our house in the suburbs. During the course of their marriage, we had moved into a very nice house, and when my mom left Charlie, the apartment she found for us, was back in the housing projects.

I remember feeling angry and asking her, "Ma, why do we have to go back?" My mom didn't explain "the why." She said it wasn't any of my business and I didn't have a choice in the matter. I felt sad, then resentful toward her. I didn't care about going back to the house in the suburbs. I wanted to be where there was peace, and in that housing project apartment is where I felt peace.

These experiences would later shape how I viewed women who stayed in domestic violence marriages and relationships, *(especially if you were a mother)*. I viewed them as weak, selfish, enjoying being physically abused, not loving themselves or their children enough to seek help to walk and stay away from their abuser.

However, through the years of educating myself about domestic violence *(and still learning)*, I no longer hold tightly to this view, but I still have questions. I often look at domestic violence through the lens of a child's perspective, because I've never experienced it as an adult. I'm very self-ware. I understand while learning about domestic violence from the perspective of an adult being abused, I need to have more empathy and grace. I can not allow my childhood lens, to block me from assisting an adult experiencing domestic violence.

Divorced and On Our Own

Although behind the scenes in my home I was living in "hell," outside the home, in high school I was an over achiever, continuing to excel academically and in sports. I was quiet, introverted, and reserved.

I had inadvertently suppressed my trauma and metaphorically did a Harriet Tubman. I stayed focused, having an escape plan for getting out of that house, which included graduating from high school, and attending college.

My mom and stepfather divorced when I was sixteen, and once their divorce was final, my mom, sister and I moved into an apartment. Mom had to relearn and adjust to doing things on her own, from opening up a bank account in her name, learning how to write a check, to paying bills. When she was married, Charlie had previously controlled all those things, and she never had anything in her name.

She had to start all over. Literally.

I stayed the course, focusing on my studies. During high school I was a loner (*still am*) and my life revolved around school, church and the library.

After her divorce, my mom's new found "freedom" came with a renewed sense of liberation. She touted and vowed no man would ever have her in a position where she needed to depend on them. She was angry and bitter toward all men.

To my dismay, 'Operation Break Darlene's Spirit,' was still in full effect. I was still attending church services, but now catching public transportation on Sundays to get there and back. She had stopped attending and we didn't have a vehicle.

As a teenager, I was committed to God and had absolutely no shame about it. My mom thought I was weird. She felt I was too young to be committed to God and couldn't understand why I didn't have a boyfriend, why I wasn't having sex or "fun," and why I kept getting up on Sunday mornings, taking public transportation to attend a church with "phony" people who didn't even like me.

One day she asked me, "Darlene, do you like girls?"

Me: "Yeah, there cool."

Mom: No. "Like do you LIKE them?"

Me: "What do you mean like them? As in being a lesbian?"

Mom: "Yeah."

Me: No. "I like boys."

Mom: "Well, you're sixteen, you don't date, you don't go out to parties or do normal shit like regular teenagers. I think that's weird."

Me: "I'm not regular."

Mom: "Well ...What about Sean?"

Me: "What about him?

Mom: "I know how you feel about him. You don't want any birth control just in case?

Me: "Just in case of what? I'm not going to have sex with Sean or any other boy."

Now, Sean was my first love. I was sixteen, he was eighteen and definitely too fast pace for me. I was an "L-Square" and he was the "Bad Boy," but no one could tell me how I felt about him. Everyone including Sean, knew how crazy I was about him, but being in a relationship meant having sex and well... guys tend to look forward to that sort of thing. At sixteen, I wasn't ready for sex or a relationship. Sean basically treated me like a little sister. He always treated me with admiration and with the utmost respect.

Mom: I know how you feel about him, you might decide to give him some. *(she was referring to sex)*

Me: "Ma, I'm not having sex until I get married. My focus right now is graduating high school, college, get married and then have a child.You know this already; I've planned this since I was twelve years old."

Mom: "Get the fuck outta here! Can't nobody live like that and do all that waiting and shit! You weird as fuck, you know that Darlene? All you do is go to that damn church and go to school. You have a lot of book sense, but not a lot of damn common sense."

Me: "Ma are you for real? No common sense? Let's see. I'm still a virgin, don't have multiple kids by different men, I don't drink, smoke, and I've never given you any trouble. Sounds like I have plenty of common sense and if having sex with multiple boys, partying and drinking is considered having "common sense," then people can keep that definition. It's idol worship to me."

Mom: "Darlene, get out my face with that bullshit. Ain't nobody trying to hear about all that God living."

The funny thing is, I never said anything about God.

The following year, I turned 17 years old, graduated from high school and left for college that summer.

A Deeper Dive

- Describe your childhood?
- Describe your relationship with your mother?
- Where you disciplined or abused as a child? Do you know the difference between the two?
- If you have children, are you currently using the same method of punishment / disciple with them, you experienced as a child?
- Have you ever witnessed your mother in a domestic violence situation? If so, how did this effect you? How did /or does it affect your relationship with your mother? Your husband? Your child(ren)?
- Have you ever been in a domestic violence situation? If so, how do you share this information with your children, so they would not end up in the same situation?
- Are you currently in a domestic violence situation? If so, when you're alone, do you ask yourself the hard question? "Why am I still in this marriage?"
- Have you given any thought as how this is affecting your child(ren)?
- Do you understand you do not deserve to be abused? Once you have the strength and decide enough is enough, please seek immediate assistance, with trusted people and resources. (*National Domestic Abuse Hotline* 1.800.799.7233)

Key Healing Takeaways

- *I chose to serve Jesus Christ over my mother and everyone else,even though this decision brought hardship upon me.*
- *I took comfort in the following scriptures:* 1Peter 3:17 "*For it is better, if it is God's will to suffer for doing good than for doing evil.*
- 1 Peter 4:12 "*Beloved, think it not strange concerning the fiery trail which is to try you, as though some strange thing happened unto you.*"
- 1Peter 4:19 "*So then, those who suffer according to God's will should commit themselves to their faithful* Creator *and continue to do good.*
- With *regard to forgiveness,* I *forgave my mother and stepfather a long time ago. I'll go into more depth about what forgiveness meant for me in a later chapter.*

Changing the Narrative

If you had a similar childhood, describe below how you changed the narrative in your life when you had your child(ren) or how you plan to change to it.

Part Two

My Journey Begins

Lee and Darlene (circa 1991)

The Constant Love I Didn't Know I Needed

Ladies, you know how when you first meet an attractive guy, you both catch an eye contact, your heart flutters, your mind starts racing, your body starts tingling and for a brief moment, your suspended in time and it really feels freaking magical, like sparks flying and bursting fireworks?

Well...that's exactly what did **NOT** happen when I first met Lee. Not even close!

Lee and I tell people we met over money.

No, it wasn't because he was rich *(although it wouldn't have been a problem)*. It's because we actually met at a bank, named Dollar Bank.

It was the Summer of '91 and I had just graduated from College three months earlier. I was out "in the field" working on an assignment for an advertising agency, my employer at the time. I was walking, headed back to the office, when I remembered I needed stop at the bank. As I stood at the corner of the street waiting for the light to change, I noticed an ATM outside the Dollar Bank.

"Cool," I thought to myself. Now I don't have to go inside. The light changed, and I crossed the street and stood behind a man who was finishing up his transaction.

He finished and walked away (*so I thought*). When I completed my transaction and turned around, the man was still standing there just staring at me.

"Yes." I said, very annoyed.

> *"We met over money"*
> **~D.C. CONSTANT**

"Hello", he said with a smile. He was polite, but had a cigarette hanging out his mouth and I hated smoke of any kind. We exchanged names, and I took a quick second looking him over. He was gorgeous looking, smooth skin, and he had a beautiful head full of black curly hair. He definitely had swag and looked like he knew how to have fun. I thought to myself, "Darlene, I think you've found your "FUN" guy! He fits the description.

Now, the "FUN" guy role is something I created, due to my experience while I was in College. My peers viewed me as a "square" who didn't have "fun," because I didn't have a boyfriend, wasn't having sex, and rarely went to parties. They gave me the nickname "Sis. Mary." I was fine with it because my focus was graduating and besides the nightclubs and men weren't going anywhere, right? So, I decided after graduation, I would have a "FUN" guy to hang out with, until I decide to meet my "husband."

Lee: "Where are you headed?"

Me: "Back to work. It's about 20 minutes from here."

Lee: "Can I walk you back?"

Me: "Okay.

As we walked back, he asked me about my work and what I like to do.

Lee: "What do you do for fun?" He asked.

Me: Oh, "I go to church, I said with excitement."

Lee: "I mean outside of church, what do you do for fun?"

Me: "Church. Church is fun." I said looking puzzled.

Lee: "Oh, okay that's cool. Nothing wrong with that."

I shared with him how I'd just graduated from college, but I'd never been to a night club before and he was shocked. He told me he was a waiter at a private restaurant which happened to be across the street from where I worked and he DJ'd on the weekends. His job status didn't matter to me, because my plan for him was nothing more than to be the "fun guy."

When we arrived in front of my job, he asked for my number. He called me later on that evening, and we talked for hours. He asked if he could take me to lunch the next day.

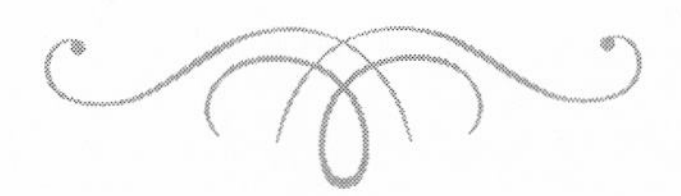

He took me to an Italian restaurant. I didn't eat Italian, nor did I eat salads. I sat and drank water. Yeah, I know, super weird. I apologized and he was really cool about it.

While we're sitting at the table, I had my pen in my hand, *(habit of being a writer)* and was subconsciously clicking the top of the it with rapid speed. I had never been on a date with a guy before and I was a bit nervous.

Lee just looked at me.

"I'm a writer, it's a habit. I always need something in my hand." I said smiling.

Lee gently removed the pen from me and placed his hand inside of mine. "How sweet," I thought. This dude was smooth right?

Nah, I think he was tired of hearing that clicking sound. LOL!

From that day foreword, we began meeting for "lunch," but never going to get anything to eat. Instead, we'd take walks every day for an hour and just talk.

So, there would be no misunderstandings, I got straight to the point with Lee. I said, "Look, I'm a virgin, I'm not having sex with you, you're not my type to marry because you don't measure up to my check list. Please understand your only role in my life is to be the "FUN" guy. Period.

He looked at me without ever responding, but still showed up the next day and each day after for our hour long walk.

Yeah. I know. I was a honest hot mess!

On our walks, we started getting to know one another and something began to happen. I found myself really liking and feeling him, but I didn't tell him.

I remember thinking, "Wow he's really a nice guy, but he doesn't have anything on my checklist. You know, the usual suspects, a degree, a high paying job, his own place, etc. *(well to be fair I was still living with my mom)*

We did go to the nightclub and I did have a lot of fun. It was weird and awkward at first, because I'd never been to a nightclub before, but Lee made me feel safe. In addition to having fun, as we continued to hang out, we connected on a deeper level, bonding and forging an unexpected, beautiful friendship.

Lee explained to me how he was looking for something and someone different. He always heard how one should get to know a person before having sex, something he had never previously done with a woman. He said he told himself, the next woman he met, he was going to give the friendship route a try and not rush into having sex, and if that approach didn't work out, he'd just go back to how he had always been doing things.

He said, "Darlene, the next woman I met was you."

Lee NEVER pressured me about having sex. I'm not saying he didn't want to have sex with me, it just wasn't the topic of conversation and my not wanting to be sexually intimate wasn't a deal breaker for him. He told me it was actually refreshing, because he was used to having sex the same day or within the first week of meeting a woman.

The beginning of our relationship mirrored the movie "Think Like A Man?" Remember the characters Lauren, played by actress Taraji P. Henson and Dominic, played by the actor Michael Ealy?

Those characters were us!

Lee and Darlene (circa 1992)

Lee and Darlene (circa 1992)

Lee and Darlene (circa 1992)

Meeting the Parents

Lee and I were now four months into meeting every day for our walks, but still had not met one another's parents and family.

When a man wants to take you home to meet his mother, it's considered a big deal and in early fall during one of our walks, Lee said, "Darlene, I talk about you a lot to my mom, I'd like for you to come by the house for dinner to meet her and my sister.

"Sure" I said, "That would be nice." Inside my head, I was like "Ummm...Darlene how did I get here? This isn't what you were looking for or had in mind. He's the **FUN** guy. Not **THE** guy."

Right?

When I arrived, his mother and sister were like, "Oh she does exist." They were curious about me, because according to his mother Judy, Lee talked about me a lot!

One of the first things Judy said to me was, "Since Lee met you, the telephone has stop ringing! No women call the house for him anymore! I needed to see who was this Darlene." We all laughed, as we enjoyed a nice dinner.

Lee's parents were divorce, so the following weekend he took me to meet his Dad. After Lee introduced me he quietly disappeared into his father's study room and left us by ourselves.

His Dad and I had a ball! We talked, laughed shared stories, and I even showed him a rough draft of an article I was writing at the time, for my upcoming news column. It honestly felt like I'd known him for years.

Lee emerged about three hours later! I believe he had fallen asleep in his father's study room. As we prepared to leave, his father gave me a big hug and told me to call him Dad. He looked at Lee and said, "Son, I'm impressed! You finally did something right!"

Needless to say, his dad was my "road dog" from that day forward!

When Lee met my mother, it did not go as smoothly as it did when I met his parents.

Upon introductions, the first thing my mother asked him was "So, what the hell are you?"

Me: Maaaaa!!!!!

Mom: "What? I said, What is he? Is he a Puerto Rican? Is he Spanish or what?"

I was beyond embarrassed by my mother's behavior. She was asking because I didn't tell her Lee was biracial. His mother was White and his father was Black.

I looked at Lee with apologetic eyes.

He gave me a smile, looked at my mother and said, "I'm human, Ma'am."

My mom wouldn't let up! She called me into our customary meeting place where we'd have our private conversations – The Bathroom.

Mom: "So, this is the guy you've been diarrhea at the mouth about?"

Me: "Mommy"

Mom: "What does he do?"

Me: "He works at a private club."

Mom: "Is he the owner?

Me: "No."

Mom: "Manger/Supervisor?"

Me: "No."

Mom: "Darlene, what the hell does he do?"

This wasn't going to be good, so I tried to play her like she was a tad bit slow and took the long route to answer. I started looking in the mirror, fixing my hair.

Me: Ma, he works at private club, as an attendant who's assigned to patrons serving them whatever they may need, he...

Mom: He's a fucking Bus Boy Darlene! I did not send you to college to bring me home a got damn Bus Boy!

Me: He's not a Bus Boy. He's a Waiter, there's a difference."

Mom: Darlene, don't talk that reverse 'pyscho babble' bullshit to me! It's the same damn thing! I swear your stupid as fuck! And where's that nice young college man, you met awhile back? What happened to him?

Me: Who, Tony?

Mom: Yeah... He was a nice young man.

Me: What about him?

Mom: "I really liked him for you. Now he's the type of man you should be with. Ya'll both on the same education level."

She was right. Tony was a very nice guy, whom I met at a local City event. He was handsome, respectable, climbing the corporate ladder, and no doubt destined for greatest.

Me: "Ma, Tony and I we went out twice, I told him about Lee and he couldn't understand how I could be remotely interested in somebody like Lee and not him, because Lee didn't' have the status or level of success he had. He told me to give him a call after I came to my senses."

Mom: Shaking her head, "I agree with him. Girl, you really need to come to your senses. You're stupid and still don't have any common sense."

Me: "Ma, everything Tony has is great for Tony, and I can get material things for myself, I retorted. Everything Tony has, he earned through his hard work. They're *his* things, not mine. So, I'm good. I don't look at him as a romantic partner, only as a friend, and I don't believe a woman should be with a man just for his "stuff" if she doesn't reciprocate his love. That's being a user. I would never use Tony or any man in that way.

Mom: "You still a dummy. But I get it. Lee is your first piece of dick and you think you all in love and shit. You're just going through a phase; it's not gone last anyway."

The truth was Lee and I had not had sex, but he already had my heart. I can't explain it. It would take a lifetime trying to. I just knew we both had something special beyond our friendship.

By Thanksgiving we were officially a couple and Lee proposed to me. He said, "Darlene I've hit the 'jackpot,' and I knew you were the one I was going to share the rest of my life with. I love you."

I was surprised and taken aback. Not that he wanted to marry me. I mean, "What man wouldn't? I thought it was too early in our relationship. I said, "Wow! That's really sweet," but I'm going to have to say no. Well... not right now."

I felt we were too young and explained to Lee, how I was getting used to being in a relationship with a man, as I 'd never been in one before and I definitely wasn't ready for marriage, but I wanted to continue exploring, growing and developing our relationship. He understood, respected my decision and never took it personally.

What was mind blowing was Lee proposed to me, and we still had not had sex! Most men preferred to 'test drive' before they made a marriage commitment.

Our Toughest Year and an Unexpected Trigger

One of our toughest trails came long before we got married, and could have easily "killed" not only our relationship, but our friendship as well.

I had this bright idea to purchase a car, even though neither one of us had a driver's license. Lee knew how to drive, but I didn't. Although we had multiple conversations about me needing to enroll in driving school, I told him I was going to buy a car anyway.

He was totally against it, you know, reminding me not only did I not have a driver's licenses, couldn't drive.

"It can't be that hard," I said, frowning up my face. "I mean I've been a passenger for years, so what's to it to drive?"

---

*Sidebar: Okay this ladies and gentleman, I will admit, this decision was clearly shows I did not have any "common sense."

Well, I didn't wait, and actually called a friend to take me car shopping. We found a dealership and a salesman who saw "SUCKER," written all over my face. He sold me a two-tone green Buick for $3,500. I only had $1,500 on me, which he gladly took and put me on a payment plan to pay the rest. I was honest about not having any insurance and not knowing how to drive a car and he said, "No problem."

When I showed up at Lee's house, *(thank God I didn't kill myself or anyone else)* I jumped out the car, ran into the house, excited to show him how we now had our own car! No more taking public transportation.

My excitement quickly dampened, when I saw the look of horror on his face!

Me: "What's wrong? I asked

Lee: "You brought a car?" He asked, in his always calming voice.

Me: "Yes." ...aaaannnnnnddddd

Lee: "Darlene. You don't know how to drive."

Me: "I know."

He stood there, shaking his head, repeating, "We discussed this. We agreed you would take driving lessons. I really can't believe you went and bought a car. This isn't like buying a dress from the department store and then taking it back."

Lee: "How much did you pay for it?"

Me: It cost $3,500, I paid $1,500 and still owe $2,000.

Lee: "How many miles does it have?"

Me: "What's miles?"

Lee: "You're really something, he said, still shaking his head. The dealership can get in trouble for selling you a car without having a license and insurance. You really need to take this car back."

When Judy found out, she agreed as well and suggested I call the dealership to make plans to return the car because what they did was illegal. I contacted the dealership and, scheduled the appointment. I also called my stepfather explained the situation and asked him to meet us there.

Once at the dealership, the salesman who sold me the car was shocked to see I wasn't by myself, and my stepfather wasted no time getting in the salesman's face.

Salesman: "Hey folks," he said with a big smile, how can I help you?

Stepfather: Getting straight to the point, "Look here, you sold my daughter this car?

Salesman: "Uh yes Sir."

Stepfather: "She doesn't have a driver's license or any insurance, and this is a Junker you sold her. He pointed at me and said to the salesmen, "Look, she's stupid. The girl is dumb and she doesn't know nothing about anything, and she doesn't owe you anymore more money either, right?"

Salesman: Smiled and said, "No sir."

Stepfather: "Good cause she isn't given you nothing else." The salesman and my stepfather went into the salesman's office, while Lee, Judy and I waited outside. When they came out, everything was taken care of and I did not hear from the dealership again.

The next day my stepfather called me on my job and said he was picking me up to take me to lunch. When he arrived, I got in the car, not thinking anything about the car dealership incident, I was excited to tell him about the things that were going on in my life and my accomplishments, my great new career, etc., and while I was speaking, he cut me off...

Stepfather: "Are you fucking that boy that was with you at the car dealership last night?"

Me: "Huh?" "What?" I was shocked!

Stepfather: "You heard what the fuck I said, are you giving him my pussy?"

I went radio silent. I began thinking. "I'm tired of him talking to me like this. Darlene, you're a college graduate, you have a great job, a wonderful boyfriend who cares about you. Tell him it's none of his business what you do with your boyfriend!"

Me: "I looked up and boldly said, "It's none of your business what I do with him!"

You would have thought I cursed at him *(which would have been justified)*. His eyes were bucked wide and while still driving with his left hand he grab my neck with his right one and yelled, "What the fuck did you just say to me!? I asked you, "Are you giving that nigga my pussy?"

I could barely breath with his hand wrap around my neck. I started crying and just like that, this college educated woman was twelve-years old again.

We pulled up to the restaurant. I don't remember ordering. I sat quietly the whole time. He began quoting scriptures, telling me I was a whore and how I disappointed God and I was no longer blessed. God told him to tell me I was going to hell. But...wait for it-- I could stop my "train ride" to hell, earn God's love back, if I stop sleeping with my boyfriend.

I remember sitting there not feeling anything. I was exhausted, but I didn't allow it to show on the outside. I wasn't even having sex with Lee, but I wasn't about to discuss anything with my stepfather. After lunch, he drove me back to my job with instructions to take heed and think about what he and "God" had instructed me to do.

When I got off work, I went to Lee's house. I shared what my stepfather said and what he did to me in the car. I was a mess and really shaken up. Lee was extremely gentle and kind, but very serious when he asked, "Darlene do you understand your stepfather has always manipulated you? The things he says to you aren't normal. Especially for a man who calls himself a Pastor."

I looked at Lee with a blank stare, because at the time I couldn't see what he was talking about. I had been accustomed to my stepfather treating me in the manner he did. It was my "normal" and it was all I knew.

Lee said, "Look, let's make a pact right here, right now with each other." He took both my hands and placed his hands on top. He look me dead in my eyes and said, "Today we're making this pact to never let anyone or anything come between us. Not my mother, your mother, your stepfather, our siblings, our family, outsiders, not even our future kids will ever come between us. If we decide we no longer want to be together, it will be because Lee and Darlene no longer want this relationship. It will never be due to outsiders. Nothing will ever come between us.

Do you agree to this PACT?"

With tears in my eyes, I nodded and said "Yes."

We were twenty-three years old, when we made that pact and it has held true for us during the last thirty years, with twenty-six of those years being married.

That evening, Judy and I were sitting in the living room just shooting the breeze when she said, "Darlene, can I ask you a question about last night at the Car Dealership?"

Me: "Sure."

Judy: "Why did your stepfather talk about you and to you in the manner he did?"

Me: "Like what?"

Judy: "His behavior toward you wasn't indictive of a father and daughter relationship.

Me: "Oh, he has always acted that way. He's only protecting me. The church I attend, all the men act that way when it comes to the women in the church. It's how I grew up."

Judy: "Hmmm...I see. Let me ask you another question. Has he ever touched you sexually?"

It was right in that moment, the flood gates opened. I remember looking at her, but actually looking past her, as all these suppressed memories flooded my mind. Untapped and unresolved emotions over took me and I let out a loud cry. It felt like a ticking-time bomb had been lying dormant within me for years, and now here's this explosion and I had to deal with the aftermath of the broken pieces, which were my scattered emotions.

For the next year, I was a total wreck! I had raw emotions, which I've never experienced before and I didn't know how to deal with or control them. I began having anxiety attacks, nightmares about the abuse, became withdrawn, not trusting, hyper-sensitive to anyone and everything. The worst part is I took these emotions out on Lee, the closet person to me and who loved me the most. It was very difficult for Lee to love me during this time.

Lee told me although he did not understand the depth of what I was experiencing emotionally, he knew in the wake of me reliving everything I had suppressed for many years, he was going to catch the brunt of my attacks, and he insisted I dealt with it and reassured me he wasn't going anywhere. He reminded me of our pact and his commitment to our relationship.

After Lee and I spoke more in depth, I decided to seek out a therapist. I told Lee; I was tired of not being able to handle all the emotions raging within me and because we were planning a future together, this was something I didn't need to drag into our marriage, but most importantly, I needed to first seek healing for myself, and it wasn't his job to "fix me" or be responsible for all my emotions.

> *"Triggers are like little psychic explosions that crash through avoidance & bring the dissociated, avoided trauma suddenly, unexpectedly, back into consciousness."*
>
> **~CAROLYN SPRING**

I sought out a licensed therapist, as I was adamant about not being "counseled" by any Pastor. I had previously tried that approach when the abuse happened by telling others in church leadership and nothing became of it, except for being blamed, shamed and told to "keep quiet."

For my deep religious folks who don't believe in therapists, this had nothing to do with me not being able to "pray" and "call on" Jesus. I believe one can have Jesus and a therapist too.

Plus, I did not trust Pastors.

Afterall, I was molested by one.

Therapy Session ~ Releasing Childhood Trauma

I was twenty-three years old, when I decided to enter into therapy. One of the best decisions I ever made in my life!

I wanted to understand and resolve the feelings and raw emotions *(at the time)* which dwelled within me, but was invisible to the outside world.

Here I was a high achiever, accomplished college graduate, on track with my career, but I needed to deal with and control the rage warring within me.

Listen, this confused the HECK out of me!

This wasn't supposed to be happening. I mean, look at all I've done. I did everything within my power by the Bible and now I'm asking God, "Why is the world I've built for myself crashing down on me? I've never felt like this before, and honestly it's disrupting the "perfect" plans I've had mapped out for my life."

I'm now sitting in a room being seen by an intake specialist for an assessment, before being seen by a therapist. I wasn't overly emotional or crying. In fact, the intake specialist was surprised how I was able to articulate precisely why I was seeking Therapy. After my intake assessment, I was given a follow-up appointment and my therapist's name.

I didn't know what to expect on my first therapy visit, but I went ready and prepared to do whatever it took to understand my emotions and how to control them. I showed up with my folder, notebook paper and pen in hand ready to take notes.

Yeah. I know. Who does that?

My Therapist, let's call her "Jane" introduced herself.

Jane: "Wow, I've never had a client come so prepared with their own paper and pen. Nice!"

After we spoke for a while, one of Jane's first orders of business was to have me stop referring to myself as stupid.

Jane: "Darlene, why do you keep referring to yourself as stupid?"

Me: "What do you mean?"

Jane: "When you speak about yourself, you keep repeating the phrase, 'I'm so stupid,' and you're not stupid. Listen Darlene, I've read what you've shared during your intake. You graduated college at twenty-one, and you've had a lot of great accomplishments to be so young. Stupid people don't graduate from college. They may do stupid things, but stupid people don't accomplish all that you have in such a short period in your young life. Do you know why you refer to yourself in this manner?"

I had been completely unaware I was referring to myself in this manner. I explained the history of my stepfather always calling me stupid, rarely calling me by my name and my mother would call me a dummy. So, it was 'normal' to me.

Jane said, every time you refer yourself by this word, I will stop you.

I was fine with it. I jotted in my notebook, a reminder to, "Stop calling yourself stupid."

Lee came to several of my sessions for support and to ask Jane how he could help me during my journey. I really thank God for Lee because I had no one else I could confide in or trust.

During our sessions, Jane asked me to choose what I wanted to disclose about the abuse I endured, and to describe in detail my experiences.

I described how I experienced emotional and verbal abuse from my stepfather. The name calling, body shaming, calling me ugly, telling me no man would ever want me and I was nothing more than a whore and a tool for the devil's use.

I pointed out to Jane specific periods in my life where certain abuse and situations had a profound affect on me and how at one point it became so unbearable I wanted to die.

The following, are specific periods in my life, I shared with Jane.

The Library

At ten years old, I wanted to know where we're babies came from. A natural, normal curiosity. I asked my mother, and her response was always, "Darlene, just don't get fucking pregnant!"

She then showed me various contraceptives, which included a condom, a diaphragm and pills as the means to not getting pregnant. This only confused me more, because I didn't understand what she was displaying and why she was angry while giving the explanation.

Since my second "home" was the library, my mom was fine when I asked if I could go and check out books, "Where babies came from."

It was the summer and I was so excited because I finally was going to know where babies came from. The library was a twenty- minute walk from our house. I passed and waved at our neighbors as I walked, then skipped as I headed to the library.

Once at the library, I looked around, walked up to the front desk and whispered to the librarian, "I want a book on where babies come from."

She gave me the biggest smile! She stepped away from her desk, returning in minutes with four age-appropriate books on how babies were born. I gave her my library card, she checked out the books and I headed back home. I remember feeling super excited and couldn't wait to read them.

Once I got back home, and my stepfather saw the books he became enraged! "What the fuck is this?" He demanded.

I was scared. I didn't know what I had done wrong, but I knew I was about to get a beating with the extension cord. The red one. I could always tell which color extension cord he would use by his tone and posture.

"Why the fuck do you have books on babies? You wanna fuck somebody?"

My face went blank, as I was paralyzed with fear. I was ten- years old; I didn't know what the word F***k meant.

"Get yo ass in the bedroom and take off your damn clothes! Now!"

By now, I'm crying, still not comprehending what I had done wrong. My mother intervened, "Charles, she just wanted to know where babies come from."

"I don't give a fuck!" he said. He was angry!

I'm now in my room naked and crying. He comes in with the extension cord, yank me up by one leg and began beating and talking to me simultaneously.

"Why. The. Fuck. Did. You. Get. Those. Books? Who. You. Wanna. Fuck. Some. Little. Boy? You. Wanna. Be. A. Got. Damn. Whore?!"

I'm wailing. I'm screaming. I'm crying. I'm calling out for my mother who never comes to stop him.

I'm bleeding on my legs and arms because the extension cord had ripped through my tender black skin. When he's done, he lets me go and I tumble to the floor.

He said, "Now go take your ass back down to that got damn library and take them damn books back! Don't bring no nasty, filthy ass books back in this damn house."

I gathered up the books. My body now covered with red bruises and I'm still bleeding. I felt shameful. I felt numb. I felt lost.

I took my time, as I slowly walked back to the library passing the same neighbors who had just seen me earlier. My bruises were visible and bloody. Everyone stared, but no one ask me questions.

As I was walking, I remember thinking, "When I have a baby and it's a girl, I'm not going to beat her when she asks where babies come from."

When I reached the library, I walked back up to the counter and placed the books down. The librarian who had checked them out earlier for me had a look of concern and horror on her face. She was clearly reacting to my bruises.

I was still in tears, my voice cracking, as I explained I had to bring the books back. She was very kind to me. She smiled and said, "Darlene, if you want to know where babies come from, the next time you come back, you can sit at the table and read the books here."

I said, "Thank you," and headed back home.

After all of that, I still didn't know where babies came from.

My Stepfather's "Call" into the Ministry"

We've always attended church.

Yes, even in the midst of all the abuse taking place behind closed doors at home, we were there every week, on time, like a MOB hit.

I loved going to church. I found solace there. I loved God as much as a child could understand His existence. It was an intangible connection I felt to Him, which was unexplainable.

I remember the Sunday morning I went to the altar to give my life to Jesus. I was eight years old. The Preacher was talking about Jesus and one day we would be with Him in Heaven. After the sermon, he invited those who wanted to see Jesus to come up to the altar. I thought to myself, I want to see Jesus one day and he really sounds like a good person, I'd better go up to the altar and let the preacher know.

I got up and walked to the altar and said, "I want to see Jesus."

The Preacher then asked me, "Child, if you believe in Jesus Christ, will you live your life according to the Bible and follow the rules and regulations of the church?"

"Yes!" I said, proudly! Thinking now I will get to see Jesus whenever I died. That was one of the happiest days of my life. But I had no clue what he meant by church "rules and regulations," I was just happy I was going to see Jesus one day.

By the time I was twelve years old, my stepfather was called into the ministry. During this period, he and my mom were at peace and my mom was so proud of him. She brought him a fancy new gray suit, in preparation of his ordination, which he wore proudly. He was ordained, licensed, and became one of several associate Pastors at the local church we had been attending for years. My mom would sit on the front row, beaming with pride.

She was proud of him being called to the ministry and being a preacher's wife. Looking back on it, I believe my mother thought his "calling" would change his behavior. I mean, isn't this what happens when your life is transformed?

Once a person adheres to their calling in the ministry, their life is transformed for the better right? They've taken off the 'old' mankind, put on the 'new' mankind and the sins they use to do; they no longer do anymore...and well...you know the rest of the church 'clichés.

One thing I do know, once you're called into the ministry, if you're not honest about your struggles and don't stay at the feet of Jesus, submitting said struggles to Him, you will stay in perpetual foolishness, making excuses for staying in your sin and hiding behind the church collar.

Not even a year had passed while my stepfather had been preaching and teaching, when a shift took place in their marriage, which became a rift and I would soon be placed in the middle.

The Other Women

It started with frequent late-night calls from various women who attended different churches throughout the city. They were never members in the church where we served.

Different women would call our home, hang up on my mom when she answered and continued to call back until my stepfather answered. When he answered, he would talk with them for a minute, then leave in the middle of the night telling my mother he needed to go and "pray" for them and he was doing "God's work."

An argument would ensue. Charlie would tell my mother she was crazy and hindering his work for the Lord. Adding insult to injury, there were times when he would still be on the phone talking with the other woman, telling them not to pay any attention to my mother's screaming and cursing because the Lord was still "working" on her and the devil had a "hold on her mind," she wasn't "anointed" and they should "just pray" for her.

During the day, especially in the summer when school was out, Charlie would sometimes take me with him when he drove to the homes of different women. As we rode in the car, he would always reach over and grab my vagina and say, "You know this my pussy, right? Remember, don't let nobody touch it!" I would have to listen to this clown give me these demonic speeches for years to come.

Once we would arrive at a woman's home, they would go into her bedroom and be in there for a while. I always had my Bible with me, so I would go somewhere to sit and read. I always read and loved the book of Matthew because of the parables Jesus taught. It's still one of my favorite books in the Bible.

Once my stepfather and the woman would come out her bedroom, we'd leave and head back home. While in the car, he would say the same thing about every one of these women, "Darlene, God told me, *(I'll call this one Janet)* "Janet is going to be my wife."

I would always be confused and say, "But Charlie you're already married to my mother and the Bible says, that's adultery...and"

BAM! The same hand which violated my body, was now popping me in the mouth, which was now swollen.

Stepfather: "Are you calling God a liar Darlene?"

Me: "No Sir." Now feeling stupid, I began to cry and tell God I wasn't calling Him (God) a liar and I didn't want Him (God) to be mad at me.

Stepfather: "What the fuck did I just say? God told me Janet is going to be my wife and it is so!"

This would go on for years with him having multiple women, and claiming God said, they were going to be his wife. He did marry one them, committing bigamy, because he was still legally married to my mother.

...and yes, he was still a Pastor and still preaching.

The Bathroom

As a child, I've always been reserved. Keeping to myself, staying in my room reading and writing. I always lived in a state fear. Fear of messing up and receiving a beating for any little thing, because nothing was ever good enough.

One evening, while I was in my bedroom reading a book my step father yelled out to me. "Darlene, bring your ass here!"

I jumped off my bed and went toward his voice, which was coming from the bathroom. I stood outside the door.

"Yes, Sir," I said.

"Open the damn door and come in here," he said angrily. Now what did I do wrong? I thought.

I walked in. "Yes, Sir."

He began to talk about how God was disappointed in me, *(according to him, God was always "disappointed" with me about something)* because I had a crush on the boy who lived next door.

I began to tense up, and looking around making sure I didn't make eye contact with him. I instead fixed my eyes on the blue Jack and Jill sink.

"Do you like that little boy next door Darlene?" He asked, angrily. I began shaking out of fear and didn't answer.

"God already told me you like the boy. Now pull your pants down. God said I need to make sure you're still a virgin."

I stood frozen. I heard what he said, but I was confused as to why God would tell him I needed to pull my pants down.

"Pull your damn pants down now!" he yelled. I slowly obeyed.

He then took his fingers and stuck it up my vagina. I remember feeling sick, filthy and dirty.

When he was done, I vomited in the toilet and he admonished me and asked, "Why did you do that? I didn't do anything wrong to you!"

He then repeated to me what he had been telling me since I was six years old. "Darlene, you are one ugly little girl you know that? No man will ever want you. And all that writing you do ain't good either. You're going to grow up writing porn books and be a whore just like your mother."

I was about 12 or 13 years old. I had no clue what porn was, let alone a whore.

He would assault my vagina with his fingers again on three separate occasions, while quoting scriptures to justify the molestation. He'd tell me God told him to do it and that my pussy belonged to him (Stepfather) and to always remember, I'd better not allow anyone one to touch it!

Imagine me as a child having to listen to him preach on Sunday to the congregation about living a righteous life for Jesus Christ or they would lift their eyes up in hell. Watching him sweating out his suit, from running around the church being dramatic and theatrical, then coming home from church only to be subjected to his abuse?

The hypocrisy of it all.

Go figure.

A House Divided and In Turmoil

Our house was always full of contention.

My stepfather was beyond blatant with his disrespect for my mother. We would go to church, hear him preach, only to return home to hear them argue continuously over the women he kept leaving his marital bed for in the middle of the night, under the guise of going to their homes to 'pray' for them, because again, he was doing "God's work."

My mom would say, "Charles, I'm no damn fool! There's nowhere in that damn Bible it says to leave your wife in the middle of the fucking night to go and pray for some bitch! You're a fucking hypocrite! Preaching in the pulpit, fucking bitches and you're not living right your damn self!"

He would always retort, "Florence shut the hell up! You're not even all the way saved. *(Church folk use this term when they feel they're more superior than others, it's a manipulation and control tactic*) I'm helping these women out with their kids, who are troubled and in need of prayer. You don't understand because the devil got your mind and you don't even know how to pray.

They would go back and forth for hours. He had stopped physically abusing her a few years before he was ordained. Not because he had 'found' religion, but because a judge told him, "If you hit your wife one more time, you're going to do time for me!!!" He never hit her again, but the verbal and emotional abuse continued.

The straw that broke the camel's back for my mom, was one Sunday while my stepfather was preaching, one of his mistresses came to church and she sat on the front row right next to my mother. When my mom found out who the lady was, she lost it, and stopped attending church altogether.

I continued to attend church, because my relationship with God had nothing to do with what the two of them were going through. However, my mother didn't see this way. When she left the church, and I didn't follow her lead, she was furious and called me a traitor. She felt I should have done the same.

I stood my ground, telling my mom how much I loved going to church and she would remind me that "Charles wasn't my real father and how 'those fake ass people at the church didn't give a fuck about me.' She harped on how she was my mother and how dare I betray her. When I did not denounce my belief in God, and the church, she began to see me as an enemy.

When my mother stopped attending church, my stepfather would tell her she needed to come back and be "seen" with him, because he was tired of telling people she wasn't "feeling well" and how embarrassing it was for him, she was no longer attending and sitting on the front row. He said, "After all, what are the people going to think?"

My mom looked him in the face and said, "Charles, fuck you, fuck that church and all those phony ass motherfuckers sitting up in there. Do you really think I give a fuck what they think about me? Why don't you tell them the truth? You preach in the pulpit about God, and leave church to go and fuck your whores.

As a matter of fact, have one of your bitches sit on the front row, because you playing with God. You ain't living right and I'm not sitting my black ass up there being phony. I don't play with God!"

After my mom spoke her mind, he never asked her again. What did he do? He put me in her position as a "surrogate."

Not only did my mother stop attending church, she stopped being his wife. She no longer cooked, (not for him anyway) fixed his lunch or had anything to do with him.

The front seat in the car reserved for my mother, he now made me sit in her place, even when I tried sitting in the backseat, he would yell at me to get in the front. I also had to start getting up at five in the morning to fix his lunch for work.

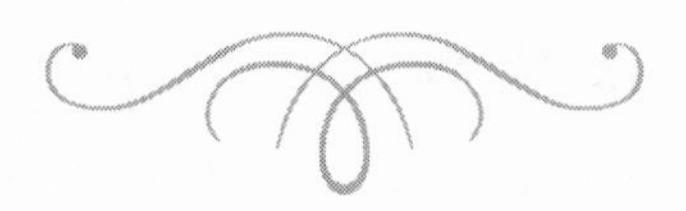

I don't remember how long it was before I told my mother what my stepfather had done to me on those occasions in the bathroom, but I do remember her response like it was yesterday.

We were all in the kitchen. My mom, sister and stepfather and I said "Mommy, I have something to tell you."

Mom: "What?"

I remember having my head down looking at the floor. I was scared, because I didn't know what would be her reaction, but I was ready and needed to tell my mother what he done to me.

Me: "Charlie, touch me down there," I said, pointing to my vagina.

There was dead silence.

Mom: "He what?" She asked, looking confused.

Me: "He touched me down there with his fingers, in the bathroom."

At this point, my stepfather began bursting into tears.

Stepfather: "Florence, this girl is lying."

Me: "Nuh uh," I said, looking surprised because he was lying. "Yes, you did Charlie. You did it three times."

His focus was on my mom.

Stepfather: "Florence, this girl is lying on me and the devil is using her to destroy my ministry. She's nothing but the devil."

I began to plead with my mother and told her I wasn't telling her a "story." Back then, a child could not use the word "lie" it was considered a curse word, and you definitely did not use this word to describe another adult.

My mom stood looking at both of us as if she didn't know who to believe. She put him out that night.

I thought she believed me and I was finally going to be protected, until she looked at me and said, "Darlene, why the fuck would he want to touch you, when he got me? I'm his wife."

Whoa.

I know.

Image how I felt.

She walked away, leaving me standing there alone in the kitchen.

He came back the next day, and we continued on with life, as if nothing ever happened.

I Wanted to Die

Time moved on and I'm now a teenager, *(before their divorce)* still living in a chaotic environment and still catching hell from both my mom and stepfather.

Not only did my mother stop attending church, but she hated anything or anyone who represented it. She also no longer looked at me as a daughter, but treated me like I was her competition.

She continued to hold the belief I had betrayed her because I still had refused to denounce my faith. She hated how I much I was invested in the church, and every time I would come home from church she'd asked, "Did you 'play' or did you 'pray' with your stupid ass? That's why Charles touched you and not your sister, because you're such a dumbass." She would ask me this every Sunday when I would come home from church.

She was trying to break me. Break my spirit.

One Sunday, after coming home and yet again listening to my mother ramble on about this, I went to my room and began talking to God. I told Him I couldn't do this anymore and I wanted to die.

My exact prayer was: "Hi God. How are you? Hope you're doing well. God, I'm tired. I'm really tired of this and what's going on in this house. I'm hurting and I'm really tired of feeling like this. I'm tired of feeling like I'm stupid and dumb....and God, because you're all powerful, can you just take me now? You have the power to do this and I can just die right now. I'm not going to kill myself, that's not in my heart to do, plus I love myself, but you're God, you made me, so you can just take me back. I'm ready."

I closed my eyes and waited. I remember feeling calm and at peace, because God was about to take me, and the pain I was feeling, which no one could see or cared about would all be over shortly. I began to smile, because at any moment now, I was going to be with the Lord. I actually believed in that moment God was going to take me.

A few minutes passed, which felt like an hour, and I became impatient. "God, what's taking you so long? I'm ready to go. I let a few more minutes pass and I finally opened my eyes. So, you're not taking me today? Okay God, maybe you'll take me tomorrow. I'll ask you again then."

Clearly, He didn't oblige that prayer.

Confronting *the* MONSTER

As Jane listened to me pour out my heart, I felt a sense of peace from releasing years of suppressed trauma.

My weekly sessions with Jane were having a positive profound affect on me and midway through one of our sessions, I said to Jane, "I'm going to confront my stepfather about what he has done to me."

Jane was taken aback, and at first was totally against the idea. She was concerned about any unrealistic expectations I may have had with regard to hearing a confession, an apology or any type of acknowledgement from him.

"Darlene, that's a HUGH step! Do you honestly feel you're ready to confront him and what are your expectations?"

I said, "Oh Jane, I don't care if he doesn't apology or even acknowledge what happened. This is about me, not him!

I'm tired of having the nightmares. I'm tired of still being controlled by him. I hate that feeling! I don't like being controlled by him or anyone else."

Jane said, "Again, I need you to understand, this is a big step and you need to prepare for the worst, because pedophiles rarely, if ever admit, let alone apologize to those whom they have abused. Since you feel you're ready, I will support you in your decision."

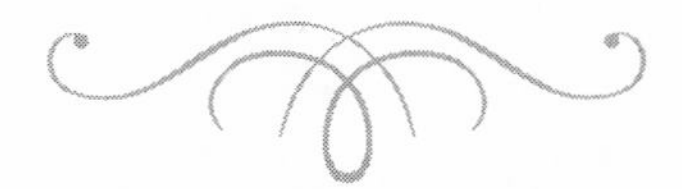

The next day I called my stepfather and went straight for the jugular. Let's just rip the band aide off, no need for pleasantries.

He answered the phone.

Me: "Hey, it's Darlene."

Stepfather: "Yeah."

Me: "I just wanted to tell you, when you molested me, fondling me in the bathroom years ago... IT WAS WRONG! And how you would sometimes kiss me in my mouth and ask me did I feel a sensation, was wrong! And how you grabbed my vagina when we would be in the car was wrong! And all those nasty things you would say to me, you were wrong!"

He was definitely caught off guard. He started to stutter.

Stepfather: "What? Girl what? Girl, your ass is crazy. I never touched you, I don't know what you're talking about.

He started laughing. You sound stupid and crazy."

Me: "Whatever, I just wanted you to know, it was wrong!" He was still laughing at me when I hung up.

It didn't matter there was no acknowledgement. I actually felt in control. I had finally taken my power back for the first time in years!

During my next therapy session, I was excited to tell Jane how I had confronted my stepfather, and how he was no longer a "GOLIATH" in my life!

When Jane walked in the room, you would have thought I hit the lottery for a million dollars!

Me: I DID IT!!! I DID IT!!! I said,

Jane: Did it? She said with a smile.

Me: Yes! I called and confronted him! I'm so proud of myself! Jane's face lit up, like a Christmas Tree.

Jane: "Walk me through the call."

I told her the call didn't last long, I confronted him about what he had done and that was it.

Jane: "What was his response?"

Me: "Oh you were right, he denied everything and even laughed at me. The call caught him off guard, he wasn't expecting it at all, but I didn't care. Like I told you, this was about my release, not me expecting anything from him."

> *"We all have a story, never allow anyone to define you by a single chapter."*
> **D.C. CONSTANT**

In total, I had therapy with Jane for about six months and toward the end I began missing sessions, going biweekly instead of my scheduled weekly sessions. Jane, of course took notice.

Jane: "Darlene, I see you've been missing some sessions, what's going on?"

Me: "Yeah, I know. I'm done. I don't believe I need to keep coming to see you anymore. I'm okay now and I will apply the tools you've given me and I thank you for listening."

Jane: Smiled. "Darlene, thats music to a therapist's ear."

Remember when I stated earlier, I had my notebook paper and a folder to place my notes in? Well, Jane had the exact manilla folder like mine and one day during a session, *(before I stop attending)* I inadvertently grabbed her folder, which had my intake assessment and treatment plan inside and she accidentally grabbed mine.

The following week, when I arrived for my session, she said, "Darlene, would you like to discuss my notes and your treatment plan?"

"Nope." I replied.

She never asked me to return her folder and I've had it for the past twenty- eight years.

Don't ask me why, because I don't know. I just never threw them away. They were kept stored in a box for years, and has now become purposeful for this chapter.

"You don't owe your family secrecy. You already carry the pain of their abuse and their lack of protection. You don't owe them your silence. You didn't deserve it. It was never your responsibility. It was never your burden to carry."

~YOLANDA RENTERIA

I'm now sharing the following diagnosis of me at the age of twenty-three years old. I had not read this diagnosis since the day I accidentally grab Jane's folder twenty-eight years ago. When I read and reviewed it for this chapter, I was like WOW! I'm so far removed from this painful experience and chapter in my life. I thanked God all over again for keeping my mind.

**My original intake session and treatment plan from twenty-eight years ago.*

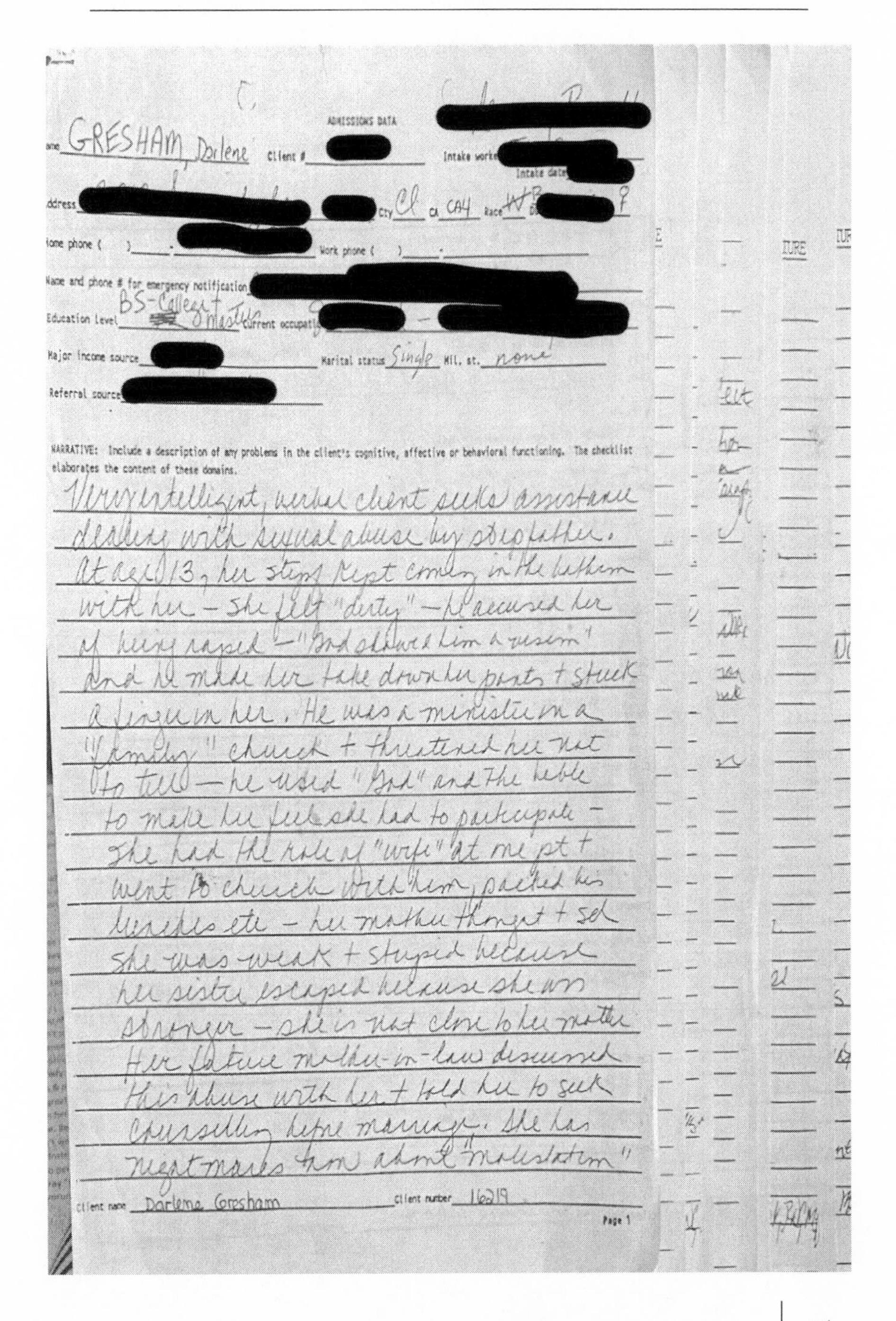

ADMISSIONS DATA

Name GRESHAM, Darlene Client # [redacted] Intake worker [redacted]

Intake date [redacted]

Address [redacted] City Cl Ca CA4 Race WP [redacted] ♀

Home phone ( ) [redacted] Work phone ( )

Name and phone # for emergency notification [redacted]

Education level BS-College + Masters Current occupation [redacted]

Major income source [redacted] Marital status Single Mil. st. none

Referral source [redacted]

NARRATIVE: Include a description of any problems in the client's cognitive, affective or behavioral functioning. The checklist elaborates the content of these domains.

Very intelligent, verbal client seeks assistance dealing with sexual abuse by stepfather. At age 13, her step kept coming in the bathroom with her – she felt "dirty" – he accused her of being raped – "God allowed him a vision" and he made her take down her pants + stuck a finger in her. He was a minister in a "family" church + threatened her not to tell – he used "God" and the bible to make her feel she had to participate – she had the role of "wife" at one pt + went to church with him, packed his lunches etc – her mother thought + sd she was weak + stupid because her sister escaped because she was stronger – she is not close to her mother. Her future mother-in-law discussed this abuse with her + told her to seek counselling before marriage. She has nightmares from about "molestation"

Client name Darlene Gresham Client number 16219

Page 1

Overview of Therapist Summary Diagnosis

It reads: Very intelligent and verbal client assistance dealing with sexual abuse by stepfather. At age 13, her stepfather kept coming in bathroom with her. She felt "dirty"

He accused her of being raped because " God showed him a vision" and he made her take down her pants and stuck a finger in her. He was a minister in a family church and threatened her not tell.

He used "God" and the Bible to make her feel she had to participate. She had the role of a "wife" at one point, went to church with him, packed his lunches, etc.

Her mother thought and said she was weak and stupid because her sister escape because she was stronger.

She is not close to her mother.

She has nightmares now about "molestation" and sees her stepfather chasing her. Her future mother-in-law said this is because she is running from herself.

She is highly motivated, but needs to stop using the word "stupid" in connection with herself.

Great relationship with boyfriend very communicative. He's her first boyfriend and sexual experience and due to the molestation and being taught by the church sex is "nasty" she continues to feel dirty about her sexuality. Lee is extremely supportive. If she doesn't want to be physically intimate, he's more than okay with it. He doesn't pressure her or make her feel shameful.

She adamantly expressed it's not Lee. It's her feelings and perception of how she views sex.

Mother did not support her when she initially heard about abuse and when she went to her Uncle's in the church whom are all ministers, they told her to "forget it" and be quiet. During our sessions, she subsequently learned one of her favorite uncles whom is also a Pastor, molested his own daughter and impregnated her three times.

She's confused about religious aspects of the abuse.

Treatment plan
Assessment impressions:
Sexual abuse Survivor

Problem: *Traumata and sequelae*
Plan: *Individual for treatment weekly for an hour*
Goal: *Increase catharsis with recovery and increase resolution of after Effects*

Objective. 1 Strengthen therapeutic alliance
Objective. 2 Provide emotional support, external validation Objective. 3 Educate sequelae associated phenomena
Objective for confront self-defeating cognitions via cognitive therapy

Problem: *Interpersonal relationships*
Plan: *Individual counseling weekly for 1 hour*
Goal: *Acquisition of adaptive interpersonal skills support network*

Objective 1: Educate constructive ego boundaries
Objectives 2: Model productive communication skills conflict resolution
Objective 3: Refer Re group therapy, group support exposure
Objective 4: Conflict counterproductive behaviors

Review Summaries

Present with History "multi-infarct" child abuse including sexual and physical abuse.

Additionally, client sustained PTSD due to prolong psychological and emotional brainwashing with the perpetrators exploiting their religious and authoritative power and positions over her.

For those who don't speak Ph.D., in simple laymen's terms the diagnoses states I sustained PTSD due to prolong psychological and emotional brainwashing by my stepfather and other religious figures who exploited their authority, power and position over me. Also, due to the trauma, I had developed a dissociative disorder.

At the young age of twenty-three, I was fortunate enough to have the insight to seek out a licensed therapist, investing in my mental health early on, and taking the first steps to my healing journey, and not allowing my past to rob me of my future.

What I was able to express in therapy, I could never express in church or with anyone who professed a belief in Jesus Christ.

Unfortunately, in my church experience, too many believers in the Body of Christ lived in a bubble (*and most still do*) as no one takes trauma or mental health wellness seriously.

There was always a disconnect, and a shifting of blame placed on the victim. In addition to victim blaming, one is always being told "It's the Devil" or "Virgin Oil" is thrown on you, while they spoke in tongues telling you to "Get Over It!" This is consistently done with lots of emotionalism, and no one having genuine concern for how you're dealing (*or not dealing*) with your pain and trauma.

Imagine being molested, rape, manipulated, etc., as a minor by authority figures in the church, whose role is to teach you about Jesus, but instead they violate you over and over again, and no one protected you? And the worst part? For many, it skewed and tainted their view of Jesus and the church as a whole. This definitely is confusing for any minor who has been raised in a church environment with this kind of toxicity.

Pastor and Author Winfred Burns II, says, "*The reality is many of us who grew up in church, grew up learning about a God that isn't the God of the Bible. We learned about a being who set people up to fail, made them work to earn his love, didn't have anything to say about our sexuality, didn't care for women, made people disabled, would rather us stay in bad marriages, was cool with chattel slavery, was ambiguous about the poor, stood by while people suffered, is jealous, doesn't have any power over the devil in the earth, and doesn't care much about creation. Oh, and his people are mean and nasty often.* THIS IS NOT THE GOD OF THE BIBLE *and we need a serious detox from our bad understanding of the Creator, so we can experience God and one another better.*"

For me, this is why I have a special place in my heart for Pastor and Church Kids (PK's and CK's) who have experienced egregious tragedies, while growing up in the church, never being able to speak the truth about their traumas, how it affected their view of God and the church, or see the perpetrator(s) held accountable for their actions.

For those of you who have experienced this, please understand it wasn't your fault and God has not forgotten you. I know it may feel like He has, but He hasn't and He Loves You!

To those who have been told by preachers and "deep" Christian folks in the church, that God allowed the perpetrator(s) to violate your body in order to make you "stronger," in Him, please reject that nonsense!

Do you really think God needed to use a pedophile, a rapist, nasty family members who commit incest, or use anyone to abuse you in any form, causing trauma, just to make you "stronger" in the Lord?"

Really?

Make it make sense!

It never ever crossed my mind to tell myself: "You know, I'm really glad my stepfather molested me, physically and emotionally abused me, because if he had not violated my body, made me feel like crap, I wouldn't be strong today."

Honestly, in my opinion, people who have this type of dismissive attitude and lack empathy, are exhibiting a slave mentally, accepting abuse. I've never allowed anyone to manipulate or minimize my reality, by telling me God used a child molester to make me "stronger," in my faith with God. To me, it's an insult to God's infinite power, as if building your faith, would only come through being sexual assaulted.

God says, For I know the plans I have you, declares the Lord, plans to prosper you and not to harm you, plans to give you hope and a future." ~*Jeremiah 29:11*

We will never know why the abuse happened. People can be unfathomably evil.

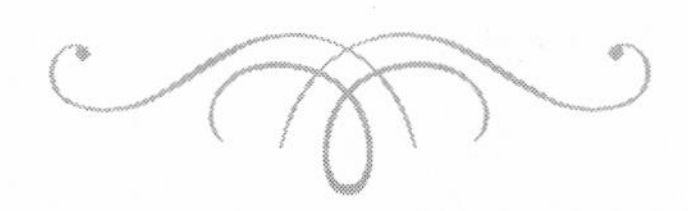

When we hold onto our trauma, it begins to manifest itself in various destructive behaviors, including, but not limited to anger, bitterness, sickness, being withdrawn, suicidal thoughts, etc. You will never forget what happened, but not seeking professional assistance to learn how to deal with the pain only allows the preparator(s) to still have control and rule over your life.

The miseducation surrounding Mental Health in churches across this country (regardless of religious affiliation) has been a huge miscarriage of justice and misunderstanding of God's will for our mental state and well-being. Especially in most African American churches. (AAC)

In my experience, the AAC culture, teaches people to be 'strong' and never have a need to speak to a licensed professional therapist. I personally have absolutely no problem with prayer, I strongly believe one can have Jesus and a therapist too!

> *"I am not what happened to me, I am what I choose to become"*
>
> **~CARL JUNG**

Think of it this way:

As a Christian, when you're physically sick, you may speak about God being your healer, but still go to the Doctor and take the medication(s) they prescribe to you for the pain.

It's no different than seeking out a therapist for your mental state and well-being. God uses people in *all* legally licensed professions.

Although going to therapy was my first step toward healing, through the years as I stayed submitted to God, He continued to minister to me, peeling back the layers of my pain.

One of the biggest pain points for me was protection. I was never protected and I learned early on I had to protect myself. As I continued to grow and mature in God, I trusted Him with "everything," except to protect me.

Having built up a wall for myself, I felt safe. It was my personal cocoon and I was comfortable and every time God began pealing back yet another layer, showing me to trust Him in the area of protection, I would get defensive with Him! It was uncomfortable yielding a mindset to completely trust God to protect me. I mean, I felt I was doing a great job protecting myself.

Then one day during prayer and meditation, I said it out loud. "God I don't trust you to protect me, because I wasn't protected as a child." After I said it out loud, I felt a sense peace. It was as if God said, "Okay, now you've gotten this out, let me minister to that hurt, let's move forward, because I have things in store for you."

As I contended with self-protection and self-defending, God began to show me the things He was after, which were a hindrance to my spiritual growth. He was elevating me, and my mindset needed to be elevated to another level of maturity in Him.

God also showed me how He had always been there protecting me, by keeping my mind, giving me an inner strength to not only survive, but to prevail and thrive from the atrocities I experienced. This inner strength kept me from blowing my brains out, or from killing those who perpetrated against and violated me.

Or both.

You know, murder-suicide.

Hey, it's been known to happen.

What Forgiveness Meant For Me

Growing up in the church, it was always confusing and vexing to hear religious leaders and people who profess to having salvation in Jesus Christ, preach and speak about forgiveness, when they were the ones causing the pain.

The onus was always placed on the victim to "forgive" and never placed on the perpetrator(s) to repent and ask for forgiveness. Too many professing Christian's are extremely dismissive when it comes to acknowledging an unjust or wrong act committed by someone in the church. They're quick to say, "You have to forgive," without ever trying to understand a person's trauma, and their pain is treated as if God doesn't care about their abuse. That couldn't be further from the truth.

To my "Super Saints," yes I know God forgives immediately, and we're taught to do the same. However, we're not God.

The process of forgiveness isn't something to be "forced" into a timeline. How you process forgiving will look different from someone else and vice versa. Never allow anyone to tell you how you should feel or grieve with the pain of your experiences.

My recommendation would be to submit your pain to God and not share what you're going through with those who prove to be dismissive toward your reality. God said, "*To cast your cares and anxiety upon Him. Just throw it on Him and let Him carry our burdens, because He cares for you*," ~1 Peter 5:7.

Forgiving my mother and stepfather was not an immediate process.

C.S. Lewis says, "Forgiveness is not a 'one-time' decision nor is it a matter of 'Forgive and Forget.' To forgive for the moment is not difficult, but to go on forgiving, to forgive the same offense every time it recurs into the memory-that's the real tussle."

For me, it meant not holding my mind hostage to reliving the memories over and over again, but releasing them along with the anger, bitterness, disappointment, resentment and the idea of how things should have been, and understanding what happened can't be undone. Mostly importantly, I needed to release them in order to grow, have peace, joy and a healthy relationship with God. Had I not done so, my life and spiritual walk would have stagnated.

How did I do this? It wasn't talking to any religious leaders or other Christian people in the church. I stayed consistently at the feet of God, with an open heart, submitting myself and casting everything onto Him.

When you decide to forgive, do it without the expectation of an apology or acknowledgment from the perpetrator(s) If you don't, you'll keep reliving what happened, and remain stagnant in your relationships with others.

My mom is seventy-years old and we're in a better place now. I no longer have this fairytale expectation of how I want her to be as a mother to me. She's never verbally apologized and she will never fully acknowledge or discuss what happened to me, and I'm long past the point in my life, where I feel I need her apology.

I'm healed.

The truth is, I will never understand how it was for her being a victim of domestic violence. It doesn't take away how she should have protected me, but I've tried to understand her as a victim with her own brokenness.

With forgiveness, comes boundaries. Forgiveness doesn't mean pretending the wrong didn't happen or believing the person should still have access to you. Although

I've forgiven my parents and other family members for the pain they've caused me; I've set boundaries when dealing with them. For an example, I don't participate in family functions, cookouts, etc., where the family pedophile who violated me *(and still violating other family members)* will be in attendance. Please don't get it twisted, this isn't "unforgiveness," but rather doing what's best for my black mental health and well-being.

When my family "protest" when I decline invitations, I tell them I owe no one, my presence and they need to respect when I say no. It's important to set and keep boundaries with toxic family members, especially when acts of sexual and any other form of abuse goes unaddressed.

For those in the religious community, instead of asking with judgement why a person isn't quick to forgive, ask "The Why" question, before hitting them over the head with the biblical scriptures. Ask "Why do they choose not to forgive?"

Stop being dismissive, with your religiosity, responding with dogma, condemning them to hell, and for the love of Jesus, please STOP comparing your pain to their pain. Their pain isn't about you. Even if you went through the same thing or something similar, it's still different, because everyone handles trauma differently. Be mature in the Lord and acknowledge their pain with empathy.

I believe in forgiveness. I don't believe in not empathizing with others in pain, as if they should just "get over it."

Those of us who are seasoned, we know God wants us to forgive. All I'm asking is that you listen with a God heart, hearing from the Holy Spirit on how to minister to God's people.

Remember, everyone's forgiveness journey to growth looks different.

A Deeper Dive

- Have you experienced sexual abuse before the age of 18 years old?
- Did you tell someone? Did they believe you?
- Are you aware of your childhood trauma? If so, was this trauma caused by someone you trusted in your family or within the church community?
- Describe how you cope with the trauma? (*i.e., counseling, self- medicated, you've never dealt with it?*)
- Do you have self-awareness with regard to your Triggers?
- If you've had counseling with a licensed therapist, what were the benefits of that experience? How have you utilized the tools your therapist recommended?
- If you haven't dealt with your trauma, have you considered seeking a licensed professional therapist?
- If you have never experience sexual trauma has someone revealed to you they had been sexually violated? (*rape, molested, incest, etc.*) Did you believe them? What did you do to assist them?
- If you kept silent, why? Do you now or have you ever felt complicit in their pain because you did not or were unable to assist them?
- Has your child(ren) ever been a victim of sexual abuse? If yes, did they tell you and did you believe them? What was your response? Did you seek counseling for you and your child(ren)?
- How are you currently protecting your child(ren) from pedophiles and other toxic family members?

Key Healing Takeaways

- *It was extremely beneficial for me to seek counseling. The epiphany I had after taking back my power, when confronting my predatorial stepfather and other religious authority figures was: I would never, ever be brainwashed again nor would my future offspring's.*
- *I appreciated God's grace for keeping my mind, and given me the inner strength as I walked through my emotional trauma. I could have very easily fell prey to the usual suspects,(i.e., drugs, alcohol, etc..) to numb my pain.*
- *I never had a "Demon" in me, but I did have religious authority figures in my life who were Demons disguise as "Pastors" and "Ministers."*
- *I have clear set boundaries, especially when dealing with those who profess faith in Jesus Christ.*
- *I didn't blame God for what happened to me, because it wasn't God that had me hemmed up in the bathroom, it was my stepfather, and I never looked at him like he was "God."*
- *I have never Trauma Bond with other people, either naturally or spiritually.*
- *I did not nor have I ever hated men. Especially black men.* BLACK MEN ARE BEAUTIFUL!
- *Most often times when a black woman has had a negative experience with a black man, she becomes bitter toward all black men. I understood all men/ especially our Black Kings were NOT like my stepfather.*
- *Besides, evil people come in every creed, shape and color.*

Changing the Narrative

Even in the year 2021, depending on one's age and the era they grew up in, there's still a stigma, within most African-American communities and churches with regard to seeking a professional therapist. This cultural mindset keeps victims from seeking the mental health wellness they need.

However, there's hope! I'm seeing a trend across Social Media platforms with Millennials who have more of an open mindset, positive dialogue, etc., which encourage African Americans to seek therapy. However, I'm not seeing the same strides being spoken from the majority of church pulpits.

If you hold a position of authority in the Church, in addition to prayer, how are you encouraging and participating in the mental health and well- being of the congregation?

If you do not have a position of authority in your church, does the leadership support and encourage you to receive professional services for your mental health & wellness beyond the church walls?

Does your religion or religious leaders have influence in your decision to seek licensed professionals for your Mental Health?

Remember, a good licensed therapist assist people on their journey to healing, improving their lives, developing cognitive and emotional skills and coping with various obstacles and challenges.

If you need to go and talk to someone, there are licensed Christian therapists available. Do your research and please know seeking professional assistance doesn't mean you're lacking in faith, in God or that you're going to "Hell."

By the way, when you make your therapy appointment, know God still LOVES YOU ☺

What Are Your Mommy Issues?

As It Relates Too How You Interact with Your Husband?

I want to explore an uncomfortable and unpopular topic as it relates to most mothers and how their daughters have related to men throughout the course of their lives, based on the parenting style and relationship they've had with their mothers.

Yes, depending on their relationship, some women can and do have mommy issues with their mother's, which in most cases are rooted in childhood trauma.

I know it's more popular and acceptable for society to discuss women who have Daddy issues (*which we will discuss later on*) however, there's a deeper need to examine the mother/daughter relationship as well.

Let's face it, little girls mimic their mother's behaviors. They don't know anything different, so when mommy is speaking to and showing her husband respect, and communicating with love, her daughter will mimic this same behavior. On the flip side, when mom is screaming, emasculating, berating and being condescending to her husband, guess what?

Their daughters will view their father/father figure in the same light, because they see mom doing it. This will set the tone and foundation for how they will interact and treat the men in their lives. It also sets them up for never taking responsibility or accountability for their part in the relationship.

"Biology is the least of what makes one a mother"
~OPRAH WINFREY

Let me explain.

Growing up, I never heard my mother, grandmother, aunties, or older female cousins, apologize to a man, about anything. EVER!

Even when it was their fault.

I've never heard any woman in my family (*or* WOMEN *outside the family*) say the following: "You know, when I look back on the time I was with my ex, this is what I've learned," or "I take responsibility for my part in the demise of my marriage/ relationship," or "I took a "deeper" look at myself and did some soul searching..." Let me stop, I'm sure I've lost most of you by now, but you get the picture and know exactly what I'm talking about.

As women, were taught from a very young age, even if on a subconscious level, not to be accountable for our actions.

The truth is, before a young girl can form her own opinion or even understand how to process her thoughts and emotions about men, *(good or bad)*, her mother's influence and ideologies about men are shaped and molded into her daughter's psyche. These can be either the mother's joyful or painful experiences. Unfortunately, it's usually the latter.

For those who've witnessed their mother's toxic behavior being displayed toward her husband or the men she dated, now that you're a wife, is it possible you've exhibited the same toxics traits toward your husband?

Whew Chile!

I know, but keep on your 'Big Girl Panties' and stay with me.

Again, this may be uncomfortable for many of you, after all discussing anything, but flattering words about mothers goes against the societal 'brainwashing,' "You only have one mother," and you should never say anything negative about her.

Unfortunately, it doesn't matter how toxic or abusive a mother may have been, or continues to be, it's still considered "taboo" to shine a light on their toxicity.

This isn't implying one doesn't love their mother, but we can't neglect and not learn from our foundation. If we refuse to expose toxic detrimental childhood parenting styles, we can miss self-sabotaging adult behavior.

In order to understand one's journey into wifehood, we must dig deep, peeling back layers of unhealthy attitudes. We must acknowledge and understand who and what has shaped our thoughts, patterns, and behaviors toward marriage and what it currently means to be a wife. We must unlearn toxic behaviors, and relearn healthy attitudes about marriage and commitment.

Reflect for a moment, the relationship your mother had with your father / father figure?

Was she loving or mean toward him? Did she treat him with respect or disdain?

Did she emasculate or uplift him? Was she a nagger? or nurturer?

If your father wasn't in your life, did your mother portray him in a negative or positive light?

If negatively, why and what did she gain from portraying him in a bad light? You're loyalty?

Did your mother ever hold herself accountable, explaining the role she played as to why she and your father are no longer together?

If you feel anger or resentment toward your father, is it because you were only influenced by your mother's side of the story?

Do you have children from a previous marriage / relationship, If so, do you speak negatively about their father to them?

If you do, what do you gain from spewing negativity? You're children's loyalty? Where can you trace this pattern of anger and behavior?

If your mother spoke positively about your father, did she explain why they were no longer together?

Did she encourage you to have a healthy relationship with your father?

Do you encourage your children to have a healthy relationship with their father?

Which of the following statements resonate with you the most as it relates to how your mother described your father or men in general?

"I just love your Father!"

"You have such a great father!"

"Your father is a great provider"

"I love being a wife to your father!"

"You have your father's beautiful spirit"

"Fathers are a gift from God"

"Your father is very supportive"

"I hate your father!"

"Your father is worthless!

"Ain't No Romance without Finance"

"I Don't need A MAN!"

" Your Father ain't Sh*T"

"Your father is a deadbeat!"

"Men ain't Sh*T"

"I just need a man to help me pay my rent!"

"Men Can't be TRUSTED!"

"Your father doesn't love you, like he does his other kids"

How many phrases can you identify your mother use repeatedly about your father or men in general while you were growing up?

How did this shape your view and treatment of men throughout your relationships, before you were married?

How does it shape your view and treatment of your husband?

These phrases are considered "contractual anger." This means, based on your mother's experience from the men in her life who treated her badly, she passed her hurt, disappointment and pain onto to you. You were learning and receiving hate from an unhealed, wounded woman.

Be honest with yourself.

If you're not married to the father of your child(ren), do you speak this way about him? What are you teaching your children and what does this say about you?

If you are married to the father of your child(ren), and you speak this way about their dad, what does it say about you?

Ask yourself, "Where's this anger and resentment coming from?" Is it possible you can trace this pattern of behavior to how you witness your mother communicate *(or lack of thereof)* with your father? Or with the other men in her life?

Everything you've witnessed good or bad, as it pertains to how your mother interacted with men, has shaped and paved your journey into your wifehood, even if you're not currently self-aware.

A Deeper Dive

- Describe your mother's relationship with her mother? Her grandmother?
- Describe your mother's relationship with her father? Her grandfather?
- Describe your mother's relationship with the other men in her family? (*i.e., brothers, uncles, male cousins?*)
- When you examine your behavior toward your husband, have you displayed any of your mother's traumatic / wounded traits? If so, what are they?
- How do you plan to rectify this behavior?
- Did your mother have a relationship with your father? We're they married? If so, how was the marriage? How did this affect you growing up?
- Did you subconsciously make a "contractual anger" agreement to carry your mother's pain and hatred for your father? Hatred for men in general?
- If so, in the words of Dr. Phil, "How's that working out for you?"

---

*Disclaimer: This isn't referring to you, if you're father abused you an any form.

Key Healing Takeaways

- *I'm thankful I didn't carry my mother's ideologies and influence about men throughout my life as I would have missed out on my Black King, Mr. Constant, the Godly man the Lord designed specifically for me.*
- *Your mother's experiences with men are just that – Hers. If you choose to keep carrier her past, viewing men through her "bitter lenses," that's on you, not the men in your life.*
- *Single women: All men are not "DOGS." If you keep attracting "dogs," it's time for self-reflection and healing.*
- *Wives, understand, there's no 'perfect husband,' as you are not the 'perfect wife,' but you both are "perfectly imperfect" as God has designed you both for one another.*
- *Always be honest with yourself and recognize your trauma and triggers. Don't allow it to keep your marriage stagnate or you from being the godly wife, God has ordained you to be.*
- *Be self-aware of not becoming defensive, deflective or feeling defeated, and allow the Lord to restore and heal you. Seeking to please God as a godly wife, is always the best way!* ☺

Changing the Narrative

Understand, it's God's desire for us to be whole, in the knowledge of our true identity and worth.

His Word states, "*We are fearfully and wonderfully made in His image,*" *Psalm* 139:14. The best way to lay hold of those attributes, is to learn His attributes, which are in the holy scriptures.

The Bible is the love story of God and His beloved creation, which is us!

Let's make sure we continue to understand this narrative!

My Daddy Issues

Relating to "Spiritual Father's"

Fathers Matter.

Period.

God created men to be husbands, fathers, providers and protectors of their families.

Fathers Matter.

I know it may sound strange for me to say, 'Fathers Matter' given I did not have a good example of one. However, no matter the evil people do, it doesn't negate God's Word, concerning Fathers, and after reconciling my pain through therapy, I refused to go through life carrying resentment, hurt, anger and believing all men were the same, because they were not. Even though I held this belief, I would soon go through yet, another spiritually devastating blow!

While in my twenties, I struggled with having a father-figure. Most women who've experienced Daddy issues, due to their trauma, tend to look for "love" and "validation" in all the wrong places, subconsciously searching out a 'father figure' in their romantic relationships with men.

I didn't fall into this trap.

I was never romantically attracted to any man who remotely reminded me of my stepfather. I had already experienced one man beating and putting me down, why on earth would I date or marry a man with those same traits as my stepfather? It was an oxymoron. Beside, I vowed my marriage would NEVER reflect my childhood.

When it came to seeking out a "Father Figure," I fell into a more sinister trap. At least that was my experience. I began seeking out a "Spiritual Father" in the form of Pastors within the church community. Now this is customary within the majority of African-American church cultures to have "Spiritual Mothers and Fathers."

Most often times, these people are not your blood relatives, and it's deemed an honor and privilege to have their guidance as they nuture and teach you in the ways of God's Word. Now, when done the biblical way, it's an extremely beneficial and invaluable blessing in the lives of those receiving this spiritual guidance.

Unfortunately, the Pastors I looked up to as 'Spiritual Fathers' weaponized my privately shared testimony against me, by sexually harassing me, belittling my gifts, demeaning me, and some spoke openly about my abuse over the pulpit.

They would gaslight me when I spoke up for myself, telling me I was "out of order" "disobedient" and of course "the devil had a stronghold on me."

It was like being in the freaking MATRIX! I was devastated!

I went before God in prayer. I was hurt, angry and resentful! I was upset because I took pride in not looking at these men like they were my stepfather. I honored them as "Men of God," had respect for the office they held, and I still experienced the B.S.

I laid it all before God.

I said, "Okay, God what's really going on here? I'm giving these men respect and honor and they want to sleep with me! Really? Then they preach, teach, become theatrical by running around the church like monkeys and treat me like I'm nothing because I reject their advances? I've seen this movie and I'm good on the 2.0 version. Lord I only wanted a father figure and I don't believe it was a bad desire to have."

I just cried and laid before God. God spoke to my heart and simply said, "I'm your Father." I stayed before the Lord as He continued to minister to my hurt, filling the void of not having an example of a good earthly father in my life.

Let me tell you what happened when I got up.

God honored my prayer and I believed and honored what God spoke to my heart. He was my father. Period.

I never again sought out any Pastor or man in the church / ministry to be anything 'spiritual' to me again. I no longer had a void or orphan complex from not having a Father.

From that day forward, to today, I've always gone directly to the Lord as my father. I do not allow any man or woman in ministry to call me their "Spiritual Daughter." I'll tell them in a heartbeat, "Call me by my name, Darlene."

This isn't meant to be taken as a sign of disrespect, but in my experience, the dangers of trusting those in authority as a "Spiritual" father, mother, etc.., opens the door for abuse of power in the church from men and women who operate out of a heart of selfishness, greed and control.

It's unfortunate there are more hirelings in the church than those who are called a Pastor after God's own Heart to Shepherd His sheep. I understand not all Pastors operate in this sinister way as my husband is a Pastor, and he doesn't operate in this manner. If he did, trust me, I wouldn't be married to him.

Listen, if you believe in having "Spiritual Parents" and they actually have the heart of God, entreat you like a son/daughter in the faith without want to have sex with you, are not sexually harassing, oppressing or trying to control your life and they truly want to see you grow in Jesus, then you're blessed and thank God for them.

...But as for me and my house? We good FAM.

God is our Spiritual Father.

A Deeper Dive

- Describe your relationship with your Father. How did he treat you?
- If you're father wasn't around, did you have a "Father Figure" in your life growing up? Describe this relationship?
- What impact having or not having a Father / Father Figure in your life, dictates how you treat your husband?
- How often do you project your brokenness about not having a father, onto your husband? What kind of man do you see when you look at your husband?
- What baggage, *(if any)* are you carrying from your father whom you perceived may have failed or abandoned you? Has this skewed your perception of God's unconditional love for you as a Heavenly Father?
- What flawed view of your father did you learn was untrue after you heard his side of the story?
- Did you pick a good father for your children?
- If you have a blended family *(you both have children from previous marriages/relationships)* what negative things are you saying to your children about their Father? Why?
- What ego driven purpose does it serve for you to bash the father of your child(ren)?
- Are you jealous of the loving relationship your child(ren's) father(s) bestow upon them?
- When you became of age, did you seek out your father to share your feelings and did you listen to his explanation?

Or have you not matured emotionally to rise to this level of communication?

- How is your relationship with your father now?
- What's the most important lesson your father has taught you?

Key Healing Takeaways

- *Although there are many great Men of God who have "fathered" others in the faith, I take great comfort and hold fast to God's word that He is my Father and He is faithful.*
- *If you don't have the love of an earthly Father, I encourage you to sit before the Lord, pour out your heart and allow Him to Minister to you.*

Changing the Narrative

Webster defines Daddy issues as a psychologically complex, pertaining to a person's relationship with their father or the general archetype of the father. This could be how daughters relate to their father or how women relate to men.

What action steps are you willing to take to heal from carrying baggage related to your daddy issues?

How are you changing the narrative in the lives of your children, so while they're g rowing up, they don't carry your pain, trauma and bitterness from not having a father? Or being bitter because their father isn't in their lives?

How are you healing today, so your children will not need therapy tomorrow?

Part Three

My Journey into Wifehood

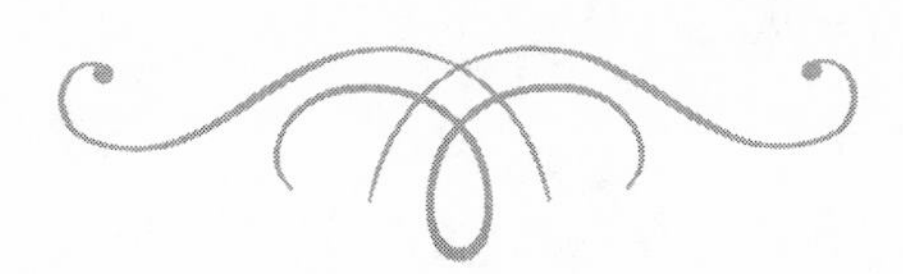

"Whatever our Souls are made of His and Mine are the Same" (Lee and Darlene 1995 Honeymoon, Pocono Mountains, PA)

Becoming "Mrs. Constant"

Lee and I married after four years of dating.

After we applied and received our marriage license, we went and got married at City Hall and went to the Pocono Mountains in Pennsylvania for our honeymoon.

The Bible says, "*He who finds a wife, finds a good thing and obtains favor from the Lord,*" *and* I love being married and being Lee's "Good Thing."

I absolutely love, honor and adore Lee. I would do it all over again in a heartbeat! He has never dishonored me and I've never been ashamed to wear his last name.

One of the most honorable things I love about Lee, is his commitment to Jesus Christ. What you see is what you get. His public and private life are parallel.

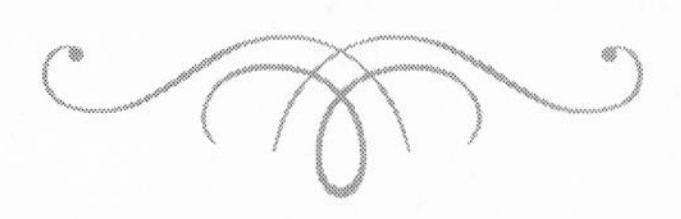

If you're a single woman, please understand marriage isn't something to be enter into lightly. I believe the high divorce rate in this country is due to people's attitudes, belief and unrealistic expectations about marriage.

I cringe when I hear people say, "Yeah, I'm getting married, but hell if it doesn't work out, I'll just get a divorce." If you have this mindset, please do not walk down the aisle. Just stay single, because with that mindset, you're not ready to be anyone's wife.

Marriage is what the husband and wife will make of it. It's a level of commitment from the heart, honored and ordained by God. A different, beautiful "adventurous" journey.

Will there be ups and downs?

Absolutely!

I guarantee it!

> *"He who finds a wife, finds a good thing and obtains favor from the Lord"*
>
> **~PROVERBS 18:22**

Marriage, is different from "shacking up." No matter how long you've lived with a man, you're still not his wife until you're married.

What does it mean to become a man's wife?

Can someone really "teach" a woman how to be a 'wife' to their husband?

I'm going to say something extremely unpopular – No,

I'm not speaking about biblical scriptures, which gives women Kingdom principals on how a wife should treat her husband.

Let me explain.

I do not believe any woman can teach another woman how to be a wife specifically to her husband.

How Sway?

For an example: A woman could have never taught me how to be "Lee's Wife," because she isn't married to Lee. It would require her to know Lee's character, his likes/dislikes, what he does and doesn't tolerate, etc..., and I've never sat down with any woman to share details about my husband, so she could "teach" me how to be his wife.

As I've stated before, being a wife isn't a 'cookie-cutter' role. What I do as a wife for my Lee, looks totally different, for what you do for your husband.

Our husbands aren't the same.

In addition to praying and asking the Lord how to be a wife to your OWN husband, you learn how to be a wife by having honest conversations with your husband, as you both decide what being a wife and him being a husband will look like for your marriage. *(this conversation can be had during the engagement stage as well)*

If you do decide to speak with wives, seeking their perspective on marriage, seek out wives who are in healthy marriages, who will share the good, and tell you how they were able to overcome their challenges. Please remember, you're just gleaning from them. Avoid wives who are always negative about their husbands, the marriage, etc. These types of wives are never accountable for their part in the marriage, and they definitely don't want to see you "happy" in yours.

#True Story

Many years ago, I was part of a women's ministry where we took turns hosting a monthly bible study at each other's home and the host always provided food and beverages.

When it was my turn to host, as the women start arriving and settling in, I was in the kitchen, gathering paper plates for the food, which had been prepared ahead of time.

While in the kitchen, one of the evangelists, *(who was single and had never been married)* walked in. "Sis. Constant, this food looks and smells delicious! When did you have time to cook? It's 6 O'clock and you get off work at 5 O'clock," she asked.

Me: "Oh, I didn't cook, Minister Constant did."

Evangelist: "What!??" She was horrified and offended?

I was caught off guard and just looked at her. I mean, "Had she not heard of a man cooking before?"

She immediately tried to admonished me and began to tell me as a wife it was my duty too cook, run his bath water, have his slippers ready when he came home from work and to make sure he didn't have to lift a finger because that's what a "good" wife does.

She was really upset.

Me: "Evangelist, with all due respect, Lee and I run our household and marriage the way we see fit and what works best for us. However, if you must know, we have what we call the "Constant Rules," and one of those rules is whomever gets home from work first cooks, that's why the food looks and smells good. Honestly, he didn't have to cook for you ladies, but that's the type of husband I have. He does the laundry because according to him, he does a better job than me, so being the "good wife," that I am, I don't get in his way. He doesn't take baths, he prefers showers, because taking a bath, then sitting in one's own filthy water is disgusting to him. He doesn't wear slippers; he loves to walk around the house in his socks. By the way, aren't you single and have never had a husband?"

Evangelist: "No, I haven't been married, but before I gave my life to the Lord, I lived with my baby's father for years. I cooked, cleaned, ironed his clothes, prepared his bath water and made sure he had money. I took care of everything.

Me: "Ohhhhh I seeeee...andddd.... he still didn't marry you? Interesting."

Evangelist: Gave me the death stare.

Me: Whelp, Evangelist, "shacking up" with a man isn't the same as being married to one and being a wife isn't reduced to just cooking, cleaning and doing the laundry. One day I'm going to write a book about it and give you copy.

Lee and I had been married eight years, and had been together for twelve, when this incident took place. This is an example of how no woman *(single or married)* can "teach" you how to be a wife to your husband, because she isn't married to YOUR husband.

Only a husband and he alone can share with his wife, his wants, needs, and desires. The bible says, "*Her husband calls her blessed and he praises her.*" Proverbs 31:28.

Not another woman.

Author D.C. Constant

What Does God Say About Wives?

God created wives to be helpmates to their husbands (*Genesis2:18*) A wife who professes Jesus Christ and understands her identity in Him isn't threatened nor seek to "take over" his God ordained given role.

A wise wife understands her husband's headship in the home, which doesn't mean she's "lesser" than and doesn't have a "voice." She understands, it's about working and striving together as a unit.

God also says, "*He that findeth a wife finds a good thing, and obtain favor from the Lord.*" ~ *Proverbs 18:22*

This scripture is often quoted, yet the power in it is often overlook. Wives are not only their husbands "good thing," but because of them, their husbands obtain favor from the Lord.

Do you understand?

As his wife YOU'RE HIS FAVOR! YES LORD!!!

YES LORD!!!

The Lord also commands us as wives to respect our husbands. We are to admire and honor them. A good wife values her husband's opinions, admires his character and is considerate of his needs, such as the need for self-confidence and the need to be needed. ~*Ephesians* 5:33

Never look at yourself as "Just A Wife!" It isn't how God sees you.

Identity – Who Are You Becoming?

Before I was married, I would listen to various married women from different social, educational and economic backgrounds speak about how they had "lost" their identity after they became married and didn't know who they were as an individual.

While in these spaces amongst these great successful women, I often asked the following question, "Is it that you "lost" yourselves or was it you didn't know who you were before you got married?"

I honestly wanted to understand what "losing" one's 'identity' looked and felt like to them in their marriages. I needed someone to go beyond telling me how they cooked, cleaned, drop off kids at various sports events, etc. as these responsibilities are SOP (standard operating procedure) when having a family, but not necessarily equated to 'losing one's whole identity.'

Is it?

After twenty-five years of marriage, I don't have this testimony nor have I ever felt this way. I've grown and changed a lot throughout the years in my marriage, but I've never felt like "I lost myself."

With regards to women feeling like they've lost their identity, Psychoanalyst Beverly Engel, author of "Loving Him Without Losing Yourself," calls it the "Disappearing Woman." This happens when women lose track of what they believe in, what they stand for, what's important to them and what makes them happy just because they happen to be in a relationship with a man.

No matter how successful, assertive, or powerful some women are, the moment they become involved with a man they begin to give up part of themselves—their social life, beliefs and values to the point when the relationship doesn't work out, they have no life to go back to.

This is why when many women divorce, it feels freeing. They have time to return to the things they love or find new interests. They don't have too "please" anyone other than themselves."

Wow! After reading this article, I felt dishearten for women who've had these experiences. It raised even more questions. This passage to me, appears to imply it's possibly the man's fault for women who feel their sense of identity has been lost in their marriage / or relationship.

I have a question.

Isn't it a woman's responsibility not to "lose" herself in any type of relationship? Where's the balance? Who said it's only the woman's responsibility to take care of everything and everyone else?

For the women who the article is speaking about, I wonder did these women communicate to their husband / partner about feeling overwhelmed, and / or having an issue with the feeling of losing their identity?

When Lee and I were dating, we were intentional to not only build a foundation bonded in friendship, we also had ongoing honest conversations about what our future would look like, our vision as a married couple, as well as our individual goals.

Marriage is about being interdependent, which involves a balance, understanding and recognizing how you both are working together, being present and meeting each other's needs (*i.e., physical, emotional, etc.*) in appropriate and meaningful ways.

Becoming "as one," in a marriage should never take away a wife's independence of pursuing her passion, dreams or purpose. Marriage with the **RIGHT** husband, should actually enhance her purpose and destiny, not hinder or take away from it.

For an example: I've always been a writer. I was Editor-in-Chief of both my high school and college newspapers, had a column in my local city newspaper, before I met Lee. When we got married, I didn't stop writing. I continued to hone in on my craft.

Lee was always buying me journals, notebooks, and anything that would enhance my writing etc., *(he still does)* because he supported me. Later on in our marriage, he would often times book me a hotel room for the weekend, because he knows how my brain works, and how my creativity flows better when I'm writing in complete silence.

Before Lee met me, he was a Gamer. It wasn't a term back then, but we've been together since the first John Madden was released on EA sports over twenty-five years ago. He's a professional Gamer now and I cheer him on and we're always laughing how the sports players on John Madden went from looking like "stick" figures to live human beings. Who would have "thunk" it!? Gaming is his thing and we respect each other's interest and space.

What are your feelings tied to when you feel you've lost your identity?

1. Marring young and having feelings you didn't have time to get to know yourself?"
2. You never wanted to be married, and married for all the wrong reasons *(ex: got pregnant, lonely, financial reasons, etc..)*
3. You have a "SUPERWOMAN" complex, and it's not that your husband doesn't assist with household chores, the children, etc. Perhaps you won't "allow" your husband to assist you, because you feel he's "inadequate?" Then do you complain when he falls back, and allows you to "do it all?"

Fill in your reason ______________________________

____

____

____

____

____

____

____

____

____

____

____

____

____

When did you realize how your identity and how you viewed yourself, was solely your responsibility and no else's?

____

____

____

____

____

____

____

____

____

____

____

____

____

Independent and Interdependence in Marriage

What does independence and interdependence look like in your marriage?

In our marriage, there's a host of marital and individual goals Lee and I have created, set and continue to accomplish in our marriage.

During the course of our marriage, we've created vision boards, and vision journals. Our vision journals are for the marriage, which represents our interdependence. It's filled with our ideas, dreams, goals, and mutually agreed expectations. Once we've achieved and reached a goal /milestone, we move on to the next one. These can be big or small.

Our vision boards, consist of our individual goals for what we want to accomplish separately from one another, which looks different from our vision journal. For example: On my vision board, my goals may have, complete next book by July 30th 2022, and underneath a detailed timeline of what tasks need to take place before the completion of the book. Lee may have something pertaining to gaming and / or ministry on his board.

There's no right or wrong way how you and your husband may keep track of your vision boards, both the marriage and individually. The purpose is to make sure you both have and maintain your passion, supporting and cheering one another on.

After twenty-five years of marriage, our vision journal has evolved, because we've grown and changed. We completed goals in our vision journal, we've pivoted and changed goals; and some goals just did not come to pass. Guess what? It was perfectly fine. The key is to continue creating and having fun while you're doing it!

One of the key things we live by in our marriage, is never getting to a point where we feel we've "arrived." We enjoy our successes, we learn from our losses and we continue setting goals, learning from one another, and always having FUN together.

The important thing is to do what works best for you and your husband. Your goals represent how you both accomplish them; they don't need to look like anyone else's marital goals.

Lee and Darlene having a blast of fun!

Communication isn't KEY... **HONEST** Communication is **KEY**

We often hear the phrase "Communication is Key." I always say: **"Honest Communication is Key!"**

When Lee and I were dating, we were honest in our communication and made it the foundation for our friendship, which transitioned into our marriage.

However, even in the honesty, I had to learn just because I was being honest, didn't mean I needed to be brutal with my delivery. I had to learn, I didn't need to cut him with my tongue, then when he'd "bleed" my only recourse was to retort "Well, I'm telling the truth!"

Yes, I was telling the truth, but I was being hurtful and unkind in my delivery. We all know, it's not what we say, it's how we say it. When you care about your husband, you will not only be willing and able to admit when you're wrong, but you will be intentional correcting your wrong doing. Mastering this level of maturity in your communication is a step in the right direction to building a solid marriage.

What's your maturity level when communicating with your husband?

Do you know your communication style? How does your husband communicate?

Do you expect him to communicate and receive information like you?

In general, most men are more task-oriented in their style of communication and most women are more process oriented. Men tend to fix and solve problems, and women tend to talk more in depth about the problem before coming to a resolve.

How does this play out in your marriage?

It's common for spouses to hear things differently when speaking to one another, which may lead to quite a few misunderstandings.

Many couples have different communication styles due to gender, age, upbringing, education, cultural differences, personality type, past relationships history and many other factors come into play when it comes to how we communicate with one another.

Regarding communication, Dr. Norman Wright termed four different communication styles, which many people fall into and believes one of the best ways to improve your relationship is by learning more about your spouse communication style, as well as your own.

Here are four types of communication styles Dr. Wright feels you may recognize.

Amplifier and Condenser Communication Style

- A condenser is one "who is most comfortable sharing little more than what is absolutely necessary."
- Amplifiers give a number of descriptive sentences as they talk, while condensers give one or two sentences.

Competitive and Affiliative Communication Style

- A competitive communicator is more oriented toward power, competition, and dominance in their communication style. Their conversations tend to be more assertive and challenging, and they prefer to make decisions on their own without much or any input from others.
- If you are an affiliative communicator, you tend to prefer, a more collaborative style of communication. You want to bring people together to work out problems.

Direct and Indirect Communication Style

- Direct communicators are rarely misunderstood, but they can risk offending their partners.
- Indirect communicators might use passive-aggressive communication when they feel upset or angry.

Hot and Cold Communication Style

- During conflict or serious conversations, there are often two ways you will approach the situation. The partner who uses a "hot style" wants to engage right away, to put the issue out there and get it done.
- If the problem isn't resolved immediately, this partner feels anxious, distressed, or preoccupied. The partner with the "cold style" doesn't do well with this intense and immediate approach. He or she needs time to think things through, but not in the heat of the moment.

Moving forward, be sure you and your husband both try to implement your communication styles and see how it improves your understanding of one another.

These are wonderful definitions and techniques on communicating, but if not applied with empathy and compassion it's all for nothing, if you aren't speaking to your husband in a respectable manner (i.e., your tone, body language, etc.)

Always keep in mind, although you and your spouse may communicate differently, speaking honestly with respect and honor should be the common denominator, which will lead you on a path to having a healthy, happy marital relationship.

The Dirty "S" Word

"Wives, submit yourselves unto your own husbands, as unto the Lord. For the husband is the head of the church and he is the savior of the body."

No. The "S" doesn't stand for Sex.

It stands for Submission.

Let's just dive right into it shall we?

For many wives and even single women, hearing the word "submission" sounds like fingernails running across a chalkboard.

Cringe worthy to say the least.

Why do the words 'wife' and 'submission' tend to have a negative connotation?

For some, I believe this word breeds contempt due to perhaps an abuse of power wielded against them by the men in their lives, perhaps their fathers, brothers, an ex-husband, or a male lover. The experience they had with these men who did not show them honor, left a bad taste in their mouths.

How did we get to the place where the word submission is equated with abuse, dominance and dogma, because this isn't God's definition of submission as it refers to wives.

When we align ourselves with humility, understanding and obedience, to God's word and His principals of submission, we will see His blessings flowing within our marriages.

There are many myths regarding what submission is and isn't and we must unlearn and relearn God's perspective on submission as it pertains to wives. In Marriage Trac, Nancy DeMoss Wolgemuth states:

1. **SUBMITTING TO YOUR OWN HUSBAND.** The scripture Ephesians 5:21 instructs wives to submit specifically to their own husbands, who have been established by God to serve as the head of their wives and to love them and lay down their lives for them.
2. **SUBMISSION DOES NOT MEAN A WIFE IS INFERIOR TO HER HUSBAND.** The scripture affirms both men and women are created in the image of God and therefore have equal worth, access to our Heavenly Father, sharing equally in the Holy Spirit, equally redeemed, and partakers of his spiritual gifts, equally loved and valued by God.
3. **SUBMISSION DOESN'T SUBJECT A WIFE TO A LIFE OF FORCED COMPLIANCE.** The word used in the

New Testament for "submission" refers to the order of following a leader-speaks of an act that is voluntary. In it's proper understanding of marriage, no husband should ever force his wife to submit to him through coercion or manipulation. Submission is a wife's willing decision, not only to follow him, but ultimately to follow in obedience to her Lord.

4. **SUBMISSION DOESN'T AMOUNT TO GROVELING IN SUBSERVIENCE.** A wife is not a hired maid nor an employee. Not a child, nor a second- class citizen who bows at the feet of her superior. Submission is rather joyful, glad-hearted, intelligent, loving response to your husband's God-ordained position as your spiritual head. (Ephesians 5:22-23) This doesn't mean husbands are the supreme authority over their wives. God is.

5. **SUBMISSION DOESN'T MINIMIZE A WIFE INTO MINDLESSNESS.** Being submitted to your husband doesn't doom you to a fate of blind, unquestioning obedience. You still possess valid opinions and the right to express them in a godly manner. As your husband's helper, you would be derelict in your duty not to bring things to his attention that he either doesn't see or doesn't seem to understand.

6. **SUBMISSION DOESN'T ALWAYS MEAN HUSBANDS ARE ALWAYS RIGHT.** Your husband is not God. (You know this already) He is every inch the sinner you are. (Hopefully you know this too) So biblical submission cannot possibly be based on how wise or godly or capable your husband is or on whether his style or manner, or

personality is to your liking. Bottom line- your husband is not the one who makes this pattern work in marriage. God is. God is the one to whom you and I as wives are ultimately submitted to in our marriages.

7. **SUBMISSION NEVER REQUIRES A WIFE TO FOLLOW HER HUSBAND INTO SIN.** Your ultimate allegiance and loyalty are to Christ. If your husband abuses his God-given authority and requires of you something that is contrary to the Word and will of God, you must obey God rather than your husband. However, my observation from listening to many wives in difficult marriages is that often their struggle is with being led in a way they don't prefer to go or just don't think it's best, rather than in a way the Bible and conscience forbid. It's important to distinguish between the two in responding to a husband's direction.

8. **A WIFE'S SUBMISSION NEVER GIVES LICENSE TO HER HUSBAND TO ABUSE HER.** Never. Ever. Whenever a woman is instructed in scripture to submit to her husband, there's a corresponding command for husbands to love and cherish their wives. There's no justification for a husband to abuse his wife, whether in overtly physical or verbal ways or in more "respectable" types of manipulation and intimidation-what one pastor calls "polite abuses." If you're being abused (or suspect you're being abused), you must seek help. There's nothing in biblical teaching on submission that permits such treatment.

Lee and Darlene "Always In Tune With One Another"

Can He Trust You ~ *with* His Heart?

"When a man can trust his wife with his fears- he is freed to love her without limits."
~Jason Wilson, Author of Cry Like A Man

As a wife, I want you to think back on a time when you were at your lowest point, vulnerable and you shared your most inner thoughts, feelings, insecurities and deepest wounds with a person you trusted the most. This person may have been your best friend, your mother, a close relative, or perhaps someone in your sister circle of close-knit friends.

Now, image after sharing your heart, you both had an argument / disagreement and they decided to not only share your business with other people, but they weaponized what you shared against you.

How would this make you feel? Angry? Belittled? Angry at yourself for opening up and trusting the person(s) were a “safe space,” vowing to never open up and share anything again?

Now, how do you think any husband would feel after opening up and sharing his heart with his wife, and she betrays him, in this same manner?

Most husband’s feel this way, when they aren’t able to become vulnerable, sharing their most intimate thoughts, fears, scars, insecurities, past etc..., without their wives using it as a weapon against them.

Can your husband trust you with his heart?

Can he trust what he shares with you, will stay between the two of you and not your family, friends, children, co-workers, or even his family?

Can your husband trust you with his heart?

Can he trust what he shares with you, will not be weaponized against him in future conversations to tear him down or to manipulate him to get your way?

Can your husband trust you with his heart?

Can he trust whatever insecurities he shares; you will not view him differently?

Can your husband trust you with his heart?

Can he trust you, to allow himself to break down and cry?

Wives, understand, your husband may love and make passionate love to you, which may even result in him “blowing your back out,” but it doesn’t mean he trusts you with his heart. For most men, these are two are separate entities. For your husband to trust you with his heart, means he trust you won't "crush it." This level of intimacy in a marriage is something very few wives experience with their husbands.

One of the things I love most about my marriage is the intimate level of vulnerability, nakedness and transparency we have with one another and Lee definitely trusts me with his heart.

If spouses can't have this level of intimacy in their marriages, who can they have this with?

Can your husband trust you with his heart?

Allow One Another to Grow, Fail and Learn the Lessons

As wives we're constantly changing, learning and growing...and guess what?

Your husband is too.

As you're both changing, as a wife make sure you're intentionally "walking in love," with the person your husband is becoming.

Richard Needham says, "You don't marry one person, you marry three: the person you think they are, the person they are, and the person they're going to become as a result of being married to you."

In marriage, mistakes and misunderstandings, are going to happen. You both are not going to be the same people you were when you first got married and this shouldn't be considered a negative.

We're all growing every day.

Before marriage, we're all at different stages in lives both mentally and physically and when we join together in matrimony, we both begin to learn, grow and navigate as a married couple.

I'm not the same person I was when Lee and I met me at twenty-two years old. If I were, this book would have been title: "What I Learned From My Divorce," because that twenty-two-year-old who had never had a boyfriend or had been in a relationship thought she knew everything!

Lee truly had the patience of JOB.

In marriage, you both are going to make mistakes, and have misunderstandings, and say things to one another you will regret.

Allow them to grow.

Allow them to fail.

Allow them to learn the lesson.

Allow them to mature in the areas where they need development and don't compare your maturity level in those areas where they need to grow. We all learn and develop at our own pace.

Once you've allowed your spouse space to fail, do not keep bringing up their past mistakes.

Remember a past mistake you made? How would it feel if someone kept reminding you of it?

For my wives who are believers in Jesus Christ, the enemy would love for you stay in the realm of past failures, pain and disappointments. Reliving and retelling the story over and over again, about why you shouldn't support your husband or your marriage. Let go of this merry-go-round thought process. Hold and embrace what God has shown you about you and your husband's future.

Make sure you're intentional about growing your marriage into a healthy place of maturity, by allowing and giving one another space to grow, to fail and grace to learn from the lesson.

Can You Stand The Rain?

One of my favorite love songs is by the most talented male group from my youth named New Edition. The popular song ask the question, "Can You Stand The Rain?"

'On perfect days, I know I can count on you. However, when that isn't possible, can you weather the storm?

I need someone who will stand by me through the good times and bad times ...tell me baby, can you stand the rain?'

All Marriages go through seasons. There will be mountain highs and valley lows and there will be rain. However, rain should not necessarily be viewed as a negative as it's natural and necessary for growth.

While I personally believe marriage is both spouses giving 100% of themselves, I can acknowledge there will be seasons in your marriage where either one of you can only give:

- 80/20
- 60/40
- 30/70

Can you both be present in your marriage during the raining seasons? Can you stand the rain when:

There's a job lost?

When there's financial issues?

There's depression and anxiety?

There's been a betrayal of infidelity? (*from either one or both of you*)

There's been a diagnosis of mental illness?

When sickness and health issues arise?

When he can no longer get his "pecker" up?

When one of you are suffering from a broken spirit?

When one or multiple "Deal Breakers" have been broken? Again?

Can you stand the rain of carrying one another's burdens, when one of you is weak and the other is strong?

I always ask wives, "Are you willing to **GROW THROUGH,** what you and your husband experience during seasons of rain?"

Again, rain is a natural part of life, necessary for growth, so embrace the rain. The key is to grow through your seasons of rain, to elevate your level of growth, maturity, and marriage stability.

Pastor and Author Winfred Burns II, says, "*We say on one side of our mouths, we want a loving relationship where we can experience growth and life together, yet we want to win every argument, get our way most of the time, never say I'm sorry, refuse to forgive, won't expose our wounds or go through seasons of carrying our partners burden. Yeah we're confused.*"

MARITAL COUNSELING

Speaking of Rain...

Lee and I experienced a dark storm in our marriage to the point where we both had 'stood our ground' on how we viewed a particular situation and neither one of us was willing to budge.

The issue was not related to communication, we both articulate our point very well. We were and have always been honest with one another because that's how we roll. The problem in this situation was we weren't listening to understand one another, at least I know I wasn't. I felt Lee wasn't understanding why I was feeling the way I felt, and I wasn't listening to understand his perspective on the matter.

In fairness, we would set aside time to discuss this one particular issue, only to become upset, with both of us shutting down. Then, we would "table it" to the point where it couldn't be 'tabled' anymore. Before leaving you to guess or assume, I will say only that the struggle we were experiencing did not involve any infidelity.

This struggle we were dealing with started out as a small thing, like having a "baby elephant" in the room. We knew it was there, but we could still walk around it. After a year, with no resolution, the issue had now grown into a full grown 'elephant in the room.' I suggested we go to counseling. At this time, we had been married thirteen years and it was the first time in our marriage where we had to weather this type of rain storm.

Yes, Lee and I were in ministry during this dark time in our marriage and for my "Super Saved Saints" yes we prayed, we cried and did all those wonderful things and still came to no resolve. We needed to speak with someone outside of ourselves.

Lee agreed to counseling and we both were adamant about not seeking out any Pastoral counseling. This had nothing to do with being "embarrassed," because we weren't embarrassed about needing counseling. Unfortunately, the disappointing truth was from our experience serving in ministry, we did not have anyone within clergy leadership who loved us enough to counsel us and whom we could trust to keep our business confidential.

Here's the thing.

We didn't decide to seek counseling trying to prove who was right or wrong, because that isn't productive counseling. We were seeking another Godly perspective on how to understand one another concerning one particular area in our life and to become free of the situation, to learn, grow and move forward.

It's extremely imperative, when all HELL is breaking loose in your marriage, you both are very careful of the counsel you seek, because everyone isn't rooting for your marriage.

You will need trusted people in your lives, who love you both, will not take sides and will seek God on your behalf. If you do decide to seek Pastoral counsel, make sure you won't hear it again come Sunday morning from the pulpit or from those who gossip from the church pews.

A very close and trusted friend of ours recommended a great Licensed Professional Christian Counselor, which made a world of difference!

During our counseling sessions, I intentionally made sure I was open, to hear and listen to Lee's perspective more than I had previously.

It took quite a few sessions, but I got it! ☺

The dark cloud, which hovered over our marriage was a raining season, and felt as if it wouldn't let up, and it shook us, but I thank God, it didn't break our marital 'force field.'

The 'Son' broke through!

The Happy Wife, Happy Life *Syndrome*

I grew up hearing the saying, "*If Momma Ain't Happy, Ain't Nobody Happy*," followed by laughter with the women in my family giving each other high fives and pats on the back.

I get it.

On the surface, it feels symbolic for when a wife isn't happy then no one in the house can be happy which translate to everyone in the house will suffer.

I personally don't like nor do I use this term.

I know for some it's just a funny saying, but for me it implies the view of a selfish wife who isn't happy unless her husband does and gives her everything she wants, as if she's the only one in the marriage who needs to be served and catered to, and her husband's needs don't count for anything.

This view is selfish and places unrealistic expectations on the husband to be responsible for his wife's ever changing emotional state, based on her definition of "happiness."

What a heavy burden for any husband to carry.

I believe most husbands love and want their wives to be happy, and being able to give her whatever she desires, makes him happy. However, I don't believe husbands want to have their needs, wants and desires sacrificed in order to make their wife "happy."

Granted each wife has her definition of what "Happy Wife, Happy Life," means, I'm highlighting, it shouldn't be based on selfishness, and entitlement.

What makes me a happy wife, is making sure when Lee comes home from work, dealing with the weight of the world all day, that walks into a "Drama Free Zone" where there's peace, serenity and his safe space, I've created for us. I never want Lee to be that husband who didn't want to come straight home after work or felt the need to sit in his car, while in the driveway before he came into the house.

This definitely would not have made me a "Happy Wife."

Our home is based on mutual respect, "Happy House, Happy Spouses."

(Lee and Darlene Constant)

Make Time for One Another
(without the kids)

A husband and wife should not have to wonder why they've "grown apart" the day their child(ren) leave the home. Often times, when couples grow apart is because they did not keep up with the maintenance during their marriage.

Please understand, in marriage, your role as parents vs your role as a husband and a wife, are two different relationships. Just as you pour into your children, raising and building them up to become healthy, strong, independent and productive people in society, you must keep and maintain that same energy with each another during your marriage.

Marriages go through many transitions throughout the years, so it's really important to be intentional about making time for one another during these transitions.

I understand the litany of responsibilities competing for both spouse's attention from the children, to work and financial obligations, etc..., While these are important, both spouses need to make sure they're making time for one another.

Lee and I have what we call "Marriage Check-Ins," which started early on in our marriage. In no particular order, it consist of, but isn't limited to the following:

- Date night once a week. We either stay home have dinner, watch a movie; or go out to a restaurant. (No electronics are allowed)
- Weekend Get-a-ways (Out-of-town or Staycation)
- Taking trips once or twice a year to a place we've never been before
- Asking each other, "Aye you, you good? You still 'happy' to be here? Anything pressing on your mind?
- Send flirting texts to each other; sometimes when we're in the same room.
- Where comfortable being in silence, while in the same room and understand there's absolutely nothing wrong.

What system do you and your husband have for "Marriage Check-Ins?" It doesn't have to look like ours. The point is to have something in place, which works best for your marriage, making sure you don't get lost in the hustle and bustle of life, neglecting to connect with one another.

It doesn't have to be fancy or expensive. You can simply start with one day a week or one weekend out the month dedicated to just the two of you.

It's about making sure you're both putting each other first, doing marriage maintenance today, so when your kids grow up and start their own lives, you won't be looking at each other like strangers.

Make Time Separately (*without* One Another)

No, I'm not trying to confuse you. Just as much as married couples should make time for each other without the kids, there should be a healthy balance of spending time apart doing things you like as individuals.

Having "me time" should never be viewed as a sign of trouble or taken personally. Spending time alone separately, will look differently for each of you, so make sure you're not dictating how your spouse should spend their "me time."

Lee and I have what we call "The Constant Rules," which have worked for us throughout the years when we each have our "me time."

You don't need to follow our 'Constant Rules,' but I recommend you and your husband make compatible "fun rules" or a list, which reflects your marriage style and your personalities.

Constant Rule#1:

Always communicate when either one of us needs space, 'me time,'etc.. Never assume we know when the other may need time to themselves.

Yes, Lee and I have been together for a total of thirty years and we're intertwined and intune like the C chord, but we still can't read each other's minds (*well not all the time* ☺)

Constant Rule #2:

Be considerate of each other's need for space when it looks different from your needs and respect, it.

Lee is a gamer and when he's playing, I know that's his "me time," and not the time to invade his space and say, "Hey babe, I've been working on an idea concept for my next book and..." No, that isn't respecting his time or his space. I can wait to discuss my new book concepts or anything else at another time, and vice versa.

Constant Rule #3

Focusing on our own projects, even when sharing the same space.

There are times when Lee and I will be in the same space, (*i.e., living room, on the patio, etc.*) sitting for hours in silence, because we're focused on our own projects. Lee may be playing his game or studying the Bible. I may be writing or creating pieces for my jewelry collection, but we're flowing separately and we don't believe something is wrong because we aren't talking to one another.

Constant Rule #4

Have a morning routine, which doesn't include the both of us.

Lee and I are up at 5:30am, and before we start our work day, Lee gets his morning coffee and watch the sports channel, and I go for my hour and half morning walk.

Constant Rule #5

In addition to having friendships with other married couples, we have separate friendships with other people.

Although Lee and I are best friends, as a married couple, it's important to foster healthy friendships outside of our marriage. We both have our own separate inner circle of friends, we connect with regularly, without each other.

Constant Rule #6

The most important rule of all RULES.

If either one of us falls asleep while lying on the couch watching television, DO NOT attempt to wake up the other person, just go to bed ~ and leave them on the couch.

Keep People Out of Your Marriage! Period!

Marriage is scarce.

Marriage is honorable in the site of God.

Due to the longevity of my marriage, I'm always asked the same question by both married and single women.

"What's the secret to staying married for so long?

Without sounding trite, my response has always been the same: "In addition to keeping God in the center of our marriage, there are three key things Lee and I have lived by for years, which has proven to maintain our healthy marriage:

1. Keep people out of your business.
2. Keep people out of your business.
3. Did I mention, to keep people out your business?

Yep, it's that simple and has worked for us the past twenty-five years of our marriage.

Keeping people out of your marriage goes for the following: Both sets of your parents, siblings, your kids, his kids, step-kids, foster kids, friends, cousins, other extended family members, BFF, Exes, baby mommas, baby daddy's, co-workers, your Pastor(s), church folks, Ronny, Bobby, Ricky, Mike...you get my point.

When our daughter Amber-Lee was a child, and felt she had a "say" or wanted to take sides in my marriage, when Lee and I would have a disagreement, we both would tell her "Amber, stay out of our marriage, what mommy and daddy have going on, has nothing to do with you." She's now twenty-three-years-old and every now and then she still needs to be reminded to stay out of our business.

I would also advise and encourage you to not listen to people who have never been married. (*I don't care if they're shacking, it's never the same as marriage*) People who haven't been married only have a "theory" of what marriage is and how they perceive how it should be done.

I relate it to sports. Let's take football.

In football, you have the players, the coach, and the spectators.

The players on the field, are in the game. They represent couples, who are in a marriage.

The coach who's calling the plays, represents "God," because God should be the only one calling the "plays" in your marriage.

The spectators represent those who are in the stadium seats, screaming and yelling at the coach and players, about "play calls" they disagree with, and feel they can do a better job, than the Coach, even though they've never coached or even played the game before.

Even though they can see the game, they're still watching from the outside looking in. This is how spectators view your marriage. They don't understand the "play call" God has spoken about your marriage, and they're upset because you're following God's direction, and not calling an audible after listening to their "advice," about what you should do in your marriage.

The bottom line is, your marriage business is between you, your husband and God, and no one needs to be given a "play by play" of what's going.

Now as a wife, I do believe wives should have someone they can confide in. Just make sure the person is prayerful, truthful, trustworthy, and want the best for both you and your husband.

Even in this, be limited in what you share, and make sure you tell the truth about your part in the situation and not just what you feel your husband has done wrong.

**(Disclaimer, this does not apply if you're currently in an abusive marriage. God does not condone abuse and neither should you. Please contact the National Domestic Abuse Hotline at 1.800.799.3224)*

Where Does The Money Reside?

Money.

Statistically, money has been considered the #1 cause for divorce.

Is it really?

Perhaps, it's the miscommunication and expectations married couples have about money management, which leads to divorce.

For example, for those who grew up poor watching their parents struggle or always fighting about money, their mindset will be different from those who grew up having more than enough. One's experience with money, will determine how they value or don't value money.

When it comes to spending the rest of your life with your husband, having an honest conversation about money is a must! No matter how uncomfortable or difficult it may seem.

Even if you're not ready to combine finances, make sure to have ongoing conversations about your personal goals, such as paying off debt, student loans, credit cards etc..., It's imperative you have a shared common goal and what works best financially for your household.

Be honest and forthcoming about your relationship with money. Are you a saver? Are you an impulsive shopper? Are you frugal? Do you have feelings of insecurities when it comes to money?

Stewart Welch, founder of The Welch Group, which specializes in fee-only investments, advice to families suggests, "The common thread for the majority of divorces is in fact money problems.

These problems can include:

1. Poor Communication about money
2. No Savings
3. Money Secrets *(i.e., secret stashes, bank accounts, hiding)*
4. Having different values about money

I never tell married couples how they should handle their finances, as each household is different. Each spouse brings different types of debt to the marriage,(*i.e., child support, student loans, credit cards, vehicle debt, business venture debts, etc.*) and how they maneuver through their finances will vary for each marriage.

I know married couples who have joint bank accounts, and those who have separate bank accounts for various reasons, and it works for their household.

A 'Piece of Paper' Matters

Growing up, I've always heard my unmarried relatives *(both men and women)* say, "Ain't no government going to tell me I need to have a piece of paper to be married, to show how I feel about the person I love. A piece of a paper don't matter!"

Why does the word marriage illicit such disdain?

Isn't it funny how no one gets their "panties in a bunch" about needing a piece of paper for legal contractual documents for the following:

- A driver's license
- Non-disclosures agreement
- Employment and independent contractor agreements
- Partnership agreements
- Consulting agreements
- Loan agreements

- When purchasing or renting a home
- When purchasing or leasing a vehicle
- Doctor's prescription
- Educational Diploma/Degrees
- Heck, even a child's school permission slip!

As a married woman, I'm presuming you're sharing various financial assets you with your husband. If you're single and reading this, you can still gain knowledge from what I'm going to share.

I want to discuss briefly, three money topics, most commonly dealt with in marriage *(or sometimes before)* Prenuptials, Bank Accounts, and Life Insurance. I'll share #TrueStories of real people, and what happens when couples do not due their "Due Diligence," by not having honest conversations around financial matters.

Prenuptials

Historically when people heard the word 'Prenup' they would only think of the rich, wealthy, and famous. However, no matter what a couples financial status, they can have one and it doesn't have to be considered a "Debbie Downer" for a marriage. It's as with any other contract, for protection.

A prenuptial agreement, commonly known as 'prenups,' is a written contract between two people before they marry legally, to detail what happens to finances and assets during the marriage, and in the tragic event it dissolves.

When I was younger, and before I was married, I thought prenups were one of the ugliest, intrusive, and insensitive documents anyone could sign. I would say, "Why would you have someone you love sign something so ugly? The audacity, right?

Well, today I'm a HUGE fan of prenups! As I got wiser I began to understand a prenup is love! Both parties should be transparent and set expectations for a successful marriage, while preventing a failed one.

Another reason I'm a fan of prenups, is due to the high percentage rate of divorces, with first marriages ending in 50%, second marriages at 60% and third marriages at 75% which has now produced a high percentage of blended families.

The truth is biological parents need to protect the inheritance of their children *(even adult children)* from previous marriages / relationships.

#True Story

Prior to my late father-in-law passing, he worked and retired from the United Parcel Service, and had gotten remarried.

He and his wife both had adult children from their previous marriages, and they both came into the marriage financially stable. To ease the minds of their children and eliminate any confusion about who would receive finances/assets upon either of their demise, my father-in-law and his wife not only drew up a prenuptial agreement, but they sent each of their children a copy, reassuring them their inheritance was not in jeopardy.

Even though they were married, they both respectfully keep their children as the beneficiaries on their 401k's, life insurance policies, etc..., My father-in-law and his wife also specified upon either one of their demise, the other spouse would receive all financial assets from what they both had built together during the course of their marriage.

After Lee and I read through the paperwork, I said, "WOW! If more people had this mature mindset, it would eliminate the need for probate court!"

Sadly, my father-n-law passed away five years later, and unlike some wives who may have tried to be underhanded (*even with a prenup in place*) and cause a ruckus, she never contested the prenup and honored her husband's wishes.

Bank Accounts

For most married couples, they have joint bank accounts, an account for bills, another account perhaps for entertainment, etc..., and some couples have separate bank accounts due to various reasons, *(i.e., child support, student loan debts, credit card debt,)* or they simply prefer to keep their finances separate.

Again, do what works best for your household. However, I would strongly suggest you name each other as the Payable on Death (POD) on any bank accounts where you do not share a signature. A POD is a bank account with a named beneficiary, who will receive the funds in the event of the account holder's death.

If you're not made the beneficiary on the account, you will not receive any funds, and the matter will be moved to probate court. Even as the wife, if your name isn't on your husband's account, funds will not be released to you. The bank only honors and recognizes whose name(s) are on the account.

For single women who are sharing a bank account with a man or just giving a man your money to "hold" in his account, you will receive nothing upon the man's demise.

#True Story

My good friend "Kay" had a boyfriend named "Rob" who proposed to her on several occasions, and she declined each of them, because she did not want to be married. When they met, Kay's only son from a previous relationship was one years old, and Rob raised him as his own.

During Kay & Rob's relationship, they lived a nice comfortable life. They had brought a home together, had multiple vehicles, he paid all the bills, etc., but they were not legally married.

Throughout the years, Kay and I would have discussions about marriage and I would ask her, "Why do you keep turning down Rob's marriage proposals?" She said, "Darlene, although Rob is an excellent provider and a great father figure to my son, I'm not ready and besides, "A piece of paper doesn't matter."

I would disagree, and tell her repeatedly being a girlfriend or even having the title fiancé is totally different from being a wife, but I respected her decision.

Fast forward sixteen years later into the relationship (*still not married*) Kay came home from work one day and unfortunately found Rob dead on their bathroom floor.

He had died from a heart attack.

This was devastating, and while she was dealing with what would be one of the most traumatic times of her life, she found out she couldn't even bury him. Not because she didn't have the money, but she wasn't his wife, so the next of kin, Rob's mother *(who never liked or connected with Kay)* took over. Not only did she take over, she never acknowledge Kay or her son whom Rob raised at the funeral.

Kay couldn't even grieve, as Rob's mother and other family members came hard at her, by hiring an attorney to try and take the house, cars, and other material items from Kay, and telling anyone who would listen, she wasn't his wife, she was just his girlfriend.

Rob had bank accounts where Kay had her monies being deposited, but her name wasn't on the account, she didn't have access and didn't know Rob's online passwords. I asked her "Did he make you the POD on any of his accounts?" She didn't know the meaning of a POD, and I said, "If you're asking me what it is, he didn't name you as a beneficiary."

Rob had insurance policies on his three children from previous relationships, but the insurance policy he had purchased for Kay, just a few years earlier, naming her the beneficiary didn't pay out, because Rob had pre-existing health conditions, which he may not have known, and that information wasn't disclosed at the time he purchased the policy.

He was also a veteran, and even though he had taken care of and verbally acknowledge Kay's son as his own, he never legally adopted him. Her son wasn't eligible for Rob's benefits, which her son could have used for educational purposes.

After sixteen years, Kay was left with their house (the deed was in both their names). She returned the cars, and other material possessions, while managing her new financial normal, as her household had been significantly reduced to one income.

She would tell me later, "Dee, you always told me a piece of paper does matter and although it's too late, I now understand."

Financial Blind Trust

#TrueStory

No, there isn't a bank institution named "Financial Blind Trust." However, it's a fitting name for spouses who are in blended families, and leave the decision making to the step-parent to handle their biological children's inheritance.

A relative of mine, (I'll call her "Sue") parents divorced when she was in her junior year of high school and her father remarried, shortly thereafter. During his marriage to his second wife, who was a professing Christian, involved heavily in her church, she appeared loving and accepting of Sue.

Years passed, and Sue's father was diagnosed with cancer. When he was diagnosed he was still of sound mind, and actually went back to work.

I had a conversation with Sue asking her if she had ever had a conversation with her father about his wishes, his assets and her inheritance, especially since she was his only child.

Sue stated they had a conversation, and her father said he had given instructions to his wife and she's "handling" it all.

After a brief pause, I asked, "Did he show you the paperwork?

"No," she responded.

When her father died, not only did her step-mother kick Sue and her now 2-year-old daughter out the home, Sue never received any financial inheritance, or anything belonging to her father. After consulting with an attorney, there was nothing Sue could do, because by law, the wife inherits everything, unless the deceased specified in legal documents what their wishes were. Her father had not left anything in Sue's name. He had trusted his wife to do the right thing.

She didn't.

I realize not all step-parents would act in this manner, however, this example along with plenty of others in blended families have become common. This demonstrates the imperative need for biological parents to understand it's their responsibility to make sure their biological children's inheritance is protected.

This isn't a slight against step-parents and it doesn't have anything to do with feeling whether a step-parent is loving or doesn't love their step-child. It's strictly about protecting the inheritance of children from previous marriages / relationships.

An Adulterous Affair

#TrueStory

My husband and I have a friend (I'll call "Alvin") who had been married for fourteen years to a beautiful woman and they had two beautiful children together. Unfortunately, Alvin had an affair with another woman, which resulted in the woman having a child born out-of-wedlock.

This was a devastating time for all parties involved and although Alvin accepted and took full responsibility for his egregious actions, the damage was done.

Alvin's wife kicked him out of the house, and to this day he's never been allowed back in their home, but she never filed for a divorce or a legal separation. Alvin suspects his wife has never asked for a divorce, due to his employment, having nice benefits and a great pension; and she still reaps the benefits of being his wife, even though they haven't lived together in over twelve years.

Over the years, when Alvin would call us, I would often ask him if he had given any thought to purchase a separate life insurance policy on himself and make his daughter, (I'll call her "baby girl") beneficiary.

He would tell me although he knew his wife hated him for what he had done, upon his death, she wouldn't dare not give " baby girl" a portion of his money.

I remember being silent for a moment, as my brain tried to process his ignorance and delusion that his wife, whom he had an affair on which produced a child, would actually consider giving this child any type of financial assistance after his demise.

I burst into laughter. "Alvin, Alvin, Alvin you really don't know much about women do you? I'm not saying there aren't women out there who haven't made sure their husband's "love child" didn't get cut off financially after their husband's death, but this isn't about your wife, or your gullible expectation to think it's her responsibility to look after "baby girl" financially, because that's you and "baby girl's" mother's job. "Honestly Alvin, don't you think that's a slap in the face to expect your wife to take care of your responsibility? Now for the wives who've found themselves in this situation and decided to make sure the child was included in the family inheritance, because it wasn't the child's fault. It's their choice, but every wife doesn't have to accept that responsibility."

Alvin and I would have this conversation for the next twelve years about why he did not feel the need to get an insurance policy. Until one day, two years ago he called me, to say he had purchased a life insurance policy (*in* X *amount*) on himself and made his now twelve-year-old daughter, who I still call "baby girl," the beneficiary.

I remember screaming, YESSSSSSSS!!!! I was so happy!

Me: "Allllvvvvvvviiiiinn, after twelve years, I'm glad you finally did that! What made you change your mind?"

Alvin: "A friend told me it was something I needed to do."

Me: Well, who's this friend, because I'd love to thank them!

Alvin: As he's laughing, "Darlene, you're the friend."

“A PIECE OF PAPER MATTERS”

These stories are way more common than one would believe, and as a married couple, it’s extremely important to have ongoing financial discussions. If you’re a wife whose currently in a blended family, and you’re the step-mother, please know it’s your husband’s duty to make sure his children from a previous marriage/relationships are financially taken care of (i.e., separate insurance policies, etc.) and this has nothing to do with you being a “loving” or “hateful” stepmother.

Whether you’re married, single with children, or in a blended family, conversations regarding financial assets, (*insurance policies, beneficiaries, 401k’s, stocks, rental property, etc.*) and material possessions (*houses, vehicles, jewelry, family heirlooms, etc.*) needs to be had. Once you have your proper paperwork in order, make sure you review and update at least once a year.

The bottom line is, biological parents need to be mature enough to have discussions on financial matters with their ex spouses, which will affect their children. Having the proper legal documentation in place, ensures all parties involved understands the wishes and expectation of each biological parent upon their demise, in regards to their biological children. This will eliminate unnecessary fighting in the courts.

Well...at least, it should.

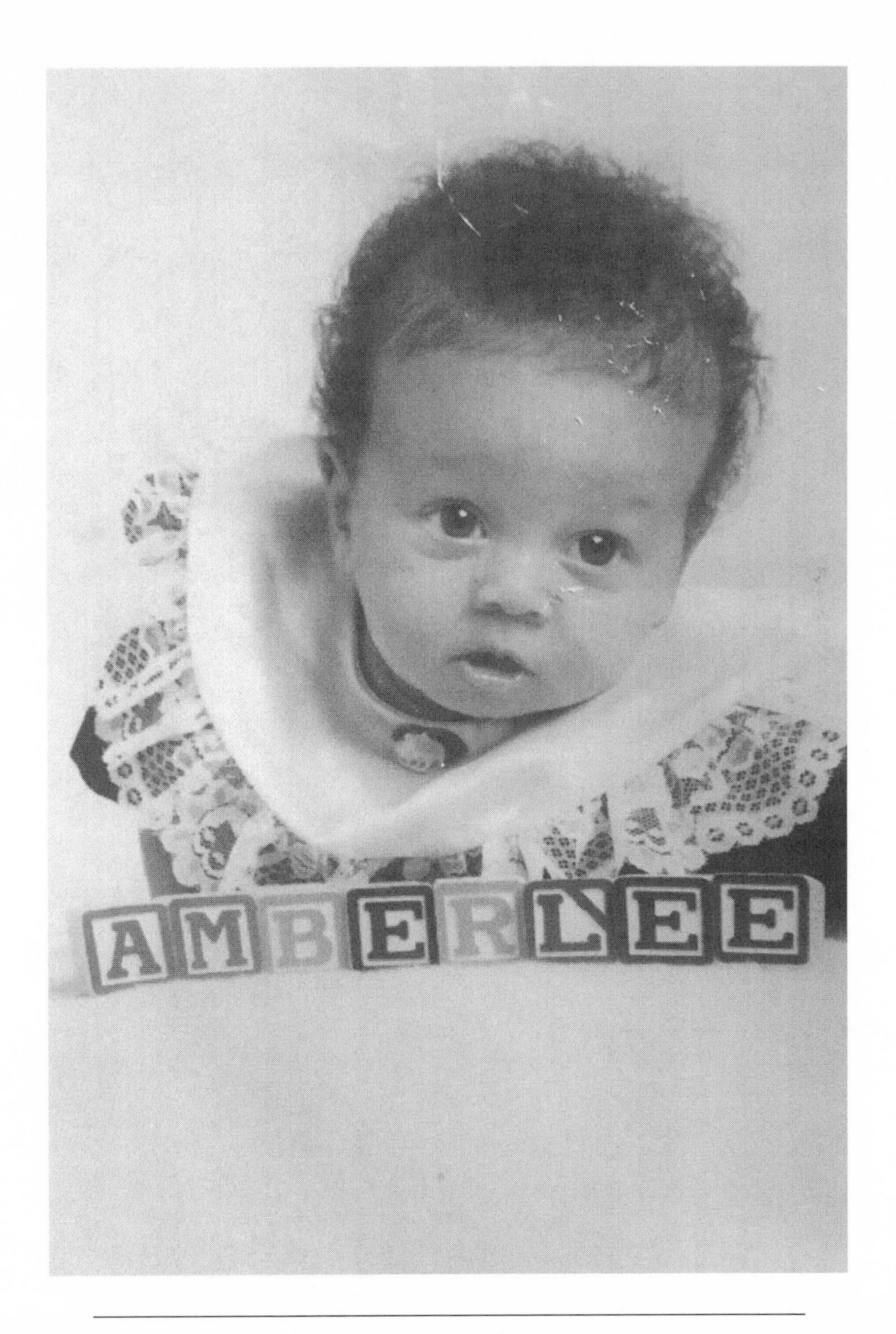

Amber-Lee Danielle Constant aka "Pretty Girl"
(3 months old)

Becoming The 'Perfect' Mother

"A mother holds her children's hands for a while, their hearts forever"

I need to apologize.

This apology is to every stay-at-home mother, past, current and future.

Let me explain.

Before I became a mother, I had a false perception of mothers who decided to stay home and raise their children instead of going right back into the workforce.

As a twenty-one-year-old college graduate at the time, I frowned upon women who stayed home after giving birth. I would always say, "When I have children, I will not be a stay-at-home mother. I mean, what do they do all day anyway? I'm a career woman."

Ouch!

Yeah. I was one those type of women.

I know. Such a stupid, thoughtless, ignorant thought process, and clearly an inaccurate one.

PLEASE FORGIVE ME. I TRULY APOLOGIZE.

For me, next to being a wife, being a mother is one of the most precious and immeasurable roles God could have blessed me with.

When Lee and I began planning for a family, the idea of being a stay-at-home mother did not register with me. It wasn't until two years after marriage, when I gave birth to our beautiful daughter Amber-Lee, my perspective changed immediately.

In that moment, I understood the importance and the blessing of being able to stay home and care for our child. I took one look at her and said, "Oh my baby will not be going to anyone's daycare!" While Lee and I worked on our transition plan for me to come off my job, my beloved grandmother Bernice, *(may she rest in peace)* took care of Amber-Lee for three months, and once I was able to leave my job, I didn't return to the work force, until Amber-Lee was in Pre-K.

It was "tight" financially, on one income, but that's what parents do. They make sacrifices for the betterment of their child's future. As parents, Lee and I were Amber-Lee's first teachers, and it was our responsibility to mold and teach her values, setting a solid foundation, which would influence and set the tone for the rest of her life. This was another reason; it was important for me to stay-at-home.

For the wives who are currently and plan to become stay-at-home moms, please enjoy every moment. I know it gets tough sometimes, andyessss the kiddos will get on your nerves, but the lessons and values you're instilling in them are invaluable.

You're truly the real MVP's!

Amber-Lee D. Constant (4 years old)

Raising An Anointed Child *of* GOD

"Train up a child in the way they should go and when they're old, they will not depart from it" Proverbs 22:6

My personal vow to God regarding Amber-Lee was, not only that she be raised in the church, but she would not be "that child" who was raised in the church all her life, but never had a personal relationship with Him. She would not be "theatrical," "gimmicky," or confused about her identity in Him. God entrusted Lee and I with the honor and tremendous responsibility of nurturing, discipling *(not beating)* correcting, guiding and nourishing her soul.

As parents, I was definitely a helicopter mom, *(for obvious reasons)* and Lee was more laid back and always the family's voice of reason, which balanced out our parenting styles.

As Christian parents, it was our job to teach our child about the Lord. We began teaching Amber-Lee her prayers, how to pray and listen to God for herself, explaining scriptures *(on a child's level)* and the importance of talking to God, honestly from her heart. We always reinforced how much God loved her and he would never stop loving her no matter what, because God's love for her wasn't based on her "performance."

Part of showing her how to have her own personal relationship with God, was when she would ask her Daddy and I for something, *(i.e., a bike, toy, etc.)* we would say, "Amber did you pray and ask the Lord about that?" It wasn't we couldn't purchase her a bike, or toy, anything else, because she never lack for anything. The point was to train her up in prayer, to understand God was *and is* the source of how Daddy and I were able to provide not only her needs, but her wants as well.

We believe in "*Train children to live the right way, and when they're older they will not depart*" *Proverbs 22:6* (NCV). For my believers in the faith, how are you raising your children and protecting their anointing and gifting, which God has instilled inside of them?

The world says, "Children don't come with a manual." However, as believers and followers of Jesus, we have the Word of God, to guide and teach us how to train and raise up our children in the admiration of the Lord.

So, how did we raise and train up Amber-Lee? We consistently did the following four things throughout her life. Please do not take this as sign that Amber-Lee never made any mistakes, that would be foolish to think. She made plenty of mistakes, but she did many things right as well. The key in her upbringing, was she learned from her mistakes, and was never brainwashed into thinking God loved her any less because of them.

(1) Lee and I had to be responsible for living an anointed Godly life ourselves.

Don't confuse living a Godly life, with living a perfect life, that's not what I'm claiming. However, we did not live a hypocritical life before her either. She never experienced her father preaching one thing in the pulpit, then experience hell at home. EVER!

We led *(and still do)* a godly life before her, which included her seeing our mistakes, flaws, and all. Most importantly, we apologized to her when we got things wrong. It was important, especially to me raising a PK *(Preacher's Kid)* for her to see daddy and I were not perfect.

Even to this day, she's a daddy's girl, and in Amber-Lee's eyes, he can do no wrong. She doesn't share the same testimony about me. ☺

When external chaos would hit our lives, Amber-Lee saw how her Dad and I handled situations, with a biblical response and the times we didn't handle things in a godly manner, we owned up to it, and discussed with her how we could have handled the situation better.

(2) Killing the ideology "Do As I Say, Not As I Do"

Think back to when you were growing up. How often did your parents use the phrase, "Do as I say, and not as I do?" Teaching you one thing, only to turn around and do it themselves? Now as a parent yourself, how often have you done this to your children?

Teaching our children one thing, and not modeling the behavior we're teaching, is hypocritical parenting at best.

I remember one of my hypocritical parenting moments.

Amber-Lee was about 10years old and while riding in the car, I was on the phone with a female relative. During our conversation we 'affectionately' referred to one another as B*tch this and B*tch that, just chopping it up laughing, casually saying this word. As we've always done since we were teenagers. I didn't think anything of it because I didn't speak this way to anyone else.

When I finished with the call, Amber-Lee said, "Ma, why do you talk like that?

Me: Confused. "Talk like what?"

Amber-Lee: "That word you were using?"

Me: "What word?"

Amber-Lee: "That B word...why were you talking like that? Her face was a look of disgust.

Me: Oh, she and I have always talked like that since we were teenagers, we weren't saying it to be mean to each other.

Amber-Lee: You shouldn't talk like that; you're acting like the people in the audience.

Me: The audience?

Amber-Lee: Yeah. The people who sit in the audience and listen to Daddy preach.

Me: Ohhhh you mean the congregation.

Amber-Lee: Yeah. The audience. You shouldn't be talking like that, because you're not in the audience.

It was in this moment, I realized I had messed up and was stuck like chuck! Ugggghh, what she said hit my gut hard. Amber-Lee was making a distinction how she viewed people who sat in the pulpit and on the front row in church differently than those who did not. Honestly, my next thought was, "Okay, the next time I'm talking to this relative, Amber-Lee won't be in the car with me."

I apologized and told her she was right. I should not have been cursing, regardless of the reason, and I reiterated it didn't matter if someone is sitting in the "audience" or in the pulpit, we should not curse, but I understood she looked up to me to be an example.

Most parents I knew, *(Christian or not)* would have beaten and cursed their child for pointing out the truth, and would have manipulated the situation, telling their child to stay out of "grown folk" business.

That's hypocritical parenting.

I was wrong. Period.

How can we empower and train up our children in the knowledge of God, if we can't admit when we're wrong? Unfortunately, too many Christian parents have a "Do as I say, and Not as I do," mentally. Many are "double agents" living one way at church, and completely differently at home and wonder why their children have absolutely no interest in God or the church.

It isn't always the 'Devil."

(3) We empowered Amber-Lee with the Word of God and never used it to manipulate or oppress her.

Many believers have favorite bible scriptures they love to take out of context or not use in its entirety to justify the taunting, mistreatment of beating their children into submission to them and God.

Ephesians 6 is a favorite scripture for overbearing parents who chose to oppress their children with the word of God. "*Children, obey your parents in the Lord, for this is right. Honor your father and mother which is the first commandment with promise: that it may be well with you and you may live long on the earth.*"

No one is arguing obedience to parents is definitely right, but instructing children to obey their parents is only one part. The scripture you usually will not hear is what immediately follows in the same sentence… "*And you Father's do not provoke your children to wrath, but bring them up in the training and admonition of the Lord.*" The scriptures were never meant to be taken out of context and used as a whipping stick to get your children to obey you in ways, which God did not intend.

Another scripture which has been taken out of context is Proverbs 13:24. "*Those who spare the rod of discipline hate their children. Those who love their children care enough to discipline them.* This scripture isn't referring to abusing your child with belts, extension cords, or anything else a parent uses to physically punish their child, but it's referring to a parent guiding their child, correcting them, teaching them right from wrong.

We must stop taunting and mistreating our children and realize they are first and foremost God's children, and their willingness to submit should be based on love and not fear. We have never used the Bible to place fear in Amber-Lee, or use it as a manipulation tool to get her to obey us or God. That's parenting out of fear. The willingness to submit should be based on a love for God and not based on being terrified of Him. God didn't want Amber-Lee to be scared of Him. We empowered her with God's Word, and she understood He's is to be reverenced, honored and obeyed.

(4) We held *(and still hold)* Amber-Lee spiritually accountable for her life.

It's a great accomplishment when our children receive excellent grades, awards, trophies, etc. However, if children who are being raised in Christian homes, can't quote, understand and expound on even the most basic biblical scriptures, something is wrong.

Amber-Lee was held spiritually accountable for reading, learning, studying and applying the word of God to her life for her personal edification. This is how she would establish and build up her faith and getting to know God, outside of me and her Dad. The earlier you begin teaching your child(ren) the word of God at their appropriate age or maturity level, the better.

From the time Amber-Lee was born I read to her from her children's bible story book. When she turned three years old I began teaching her the books of the bible, chapter and verses. At four years-old, she knew how to read and write, and every day before she went to school, we would study a bible character and then I had her write a 'mini' book report.

Yes, I was that parent ☺

When we talk about raising anointed children, as Christian parents, we must be living a godly life ourselves, so we can lead and guide them every day and not just on Sundays.

Amber-Lee, in Pre-K. Finished up her "mini book report" and was ready for school.

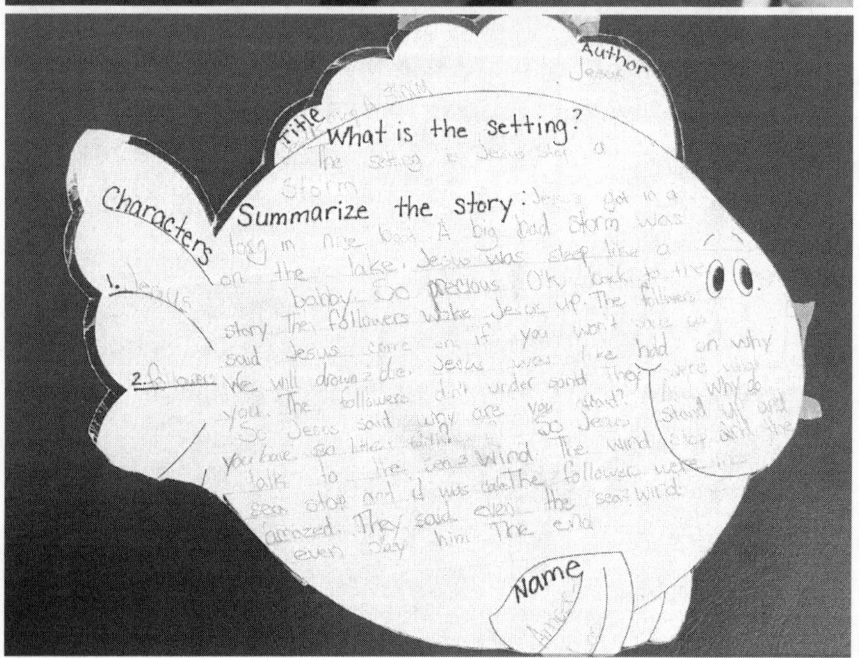

Amber-Lee and Cooper Constant

Setting Boundaries *with the In-Laws*

"For this reason, a man shall leave his father and mother and shall cleave to his wife and they shall be one flesh" Genesis 2:24) (explain this in more detail)

The 2005 movie Monster-in-Law starring Jane Fonda, who played Viola, the mother of Dr. Kevin Fields, portrayed by Michael Vartan, and Jennifer Lopez who played Charlotte the daughter-in-law, I'm sure registered with many real-life daughters-in-law around the world.

The movie depicts how the mother-in-law perceives her son Kevin's fiancé as new competition and she will do anything to destroy their relationship, hoping to make her son call off the wedding.

Her character was merciless.

When Lee and I saw this movie, I looked at him and said, "WOW, I could have written this script, the accuracy!"

When a woman is single, she often hears other women say, "Watch how a man treats his mother," as it will be an indication of how he will treat you. This was definitely true in my case, with Lee. Lee loved, respected and adored his mother, and she doted on him and in her eyes, like many mothers with sons, no other woman would love him the way she does.

Both our mothers were a blend of being a mother-in-law and mother-in-love. They would go from having no boundaries in their actions or speech toward Lee and I to being "lovey dovey," depending on the season we were in our marriage.

Lee and I both found ourselves protecting one another from our mothers and eventually had a to have a "Come to Jesus" moment with them both to establish boundaries. They both needed to be reminded we're their adult children, married, starting our own lives, and neither one of them had to like it, but they definitely had to respect it.

For Lee and I, setting boundaries with our mothers and other family members was a new concept for them. For the most part, when you're single, most families feel they can infringe upon your time, finances, etc., and when you get married, and your priorities change, many will not respect your union.

Many family members may feel they have "ownership" of you because you're their daughter, son, sister, brother, etc..., and feel the boundaries you put in place, should not apply to them and will have difficulty accepting this change.

Feelings may be hurt, but as a married couple, it's imperative to set personal boundaries in place early on.

Dr. Cloud's and Dr. Townsend's biblical approach when setting boundaries in their book: Boundaries: How to Say Yes, How to Say No to Take Control of Your Life, worked well for us when we discuss setting boundaries with our mothers. By the way, the listed boundaries, are beneficial whether you're newlyweds or have been married ten, twenty or thirty years. The important thing is to have set boundaries in place:

Look to God's Design for Boundaries

The best instructions for setting appropriate boundaries are always found in God's word, and a husband and wife are the first to learn about boundaries. "*That is why a man leaves his father and mother and is united to his wife, and they become one flesh*"(**Genesis 2:24**). In marriage, a husband-and-wife step over the boundaries set by their parents and enter into a relationship as one to build a new family.

The word "leaves" in this passage is a strong Hebrew word that means to forsake or abandon and "united" or "join" means to bond together or hold fast to. The husband and wife are to abandon the parental relationship and bond together as one in the marriage relationship. From that point, husbands and wives work together to build better boundaries with their in-laws and family.

Determine the Boundary Problem

To set appropriate boundaries, decide if boundaries are a problem for you and your spouse. Start with prayer, asking God for wisdom and guidance. Be sensitive to the needs of your spouse. Is he or she irritable when your parents or family drop in unexpectedly? Are you uncomfortable when your spouse provides your in-laws with too much information?

Openly and honestly discuss without judgment where the lines need to be drawn to maintain harmony in your relationship. "*If it is possible, as far as it depends on you, live at peace with everyone.*" (**Romans 12:18**)

Agree on the Boundaries

Once you determine there is an issue, as a couple, you work to agree on the appropriate boundaries. What is uncomfortable to one may be comfortable for the other. If in-laws dropping in unannounced is acceptable to one but not the other, try to find mutuality. You may not agree on what works and does not, but try to be open to compromise. Deciding on the boundaries together avoids future disagreements and frustration. In the end, setting appropriate family boundaries should help everyone live in harmony.

"*Starting a quarrel is like breaching a dam; so, drop the matter before a dispute breaks out.*" (**Proverbs 17:14**)

Start Small

Sitting down to dinner with his and her parents then dispensing a list of relationship commandments and rock-solid boundaries is hard to digest. Start small and add changes as the new in-law relationship grows. Keep in mind that by setting one limit, others may arise that need attention and adjustment. Like drops in a bucket, these small changes add up to a healthy, mutually respectful relationship.

"Commit your work to the Lord, and your plans will be established." **(Proverbs 16:3)**

Find Common Ground

There may be times when setting boundaries requires everyone to participate. After determining the issue then agreeing on what is best as a couple, you may need to invite those on the other side of the fence to sit at the table. When building better boundaries, the strongest borders are those protected on both sides.

"And let us consider how we may spur one another on toward love and good deeds." **(Hebrews 10:24)**

Be Patient and Flexible

Changes are complicated, and no one gets it right immediately. Once borders to the relationship are established, expect "boundary-busting" to happen. As lovingly and gently as possible reiterate your boundary lines. If the "boundary-busting" continues, stand firm and try a different approach, but be prepared to apply consequences if necessary.

"The end of the matter is better than the beginning, and patience is better than ***pride."*** **(Ecclesiastes 7:8)**

Prepare for Push Back

As in most relationships, not everyone agrees on the borderlines. Some in-laws and family members will not be receptive to changing the rules. Remain united and support each other when push-back starts. It can be easy to give in to parents, but the fallout in your marriage may be hard to mend. Be ready to hold fast to your decision for what is best for you and your spouse. If push-back and "boundary-busting" continues, do not be afraid to provide for consequences. It's alright to say, "no."

"For God did not give us a spirit of timidity, but a spirit of power, of love, and of self-discipline." **(2 Timothy 1:7)**

Share the Love

Setting boundaries with in-laws and family does not mean cutting all ties. It means putting your marriage above all relationships except God. Attending family gatherings and occasional outings does not erase all of the work you have done in maintaining separate lives. Instead, your families see that you and your spouse want to include them in your life while you remain in control of your boundaries. In some situations, sharing your time and love with some in-laws is difficult but, when possible, try to share your time.

"Above all, love each other deeply, because love covers over a multitude of sins." **(1 Peter 4:8)**

Be Direct, but Kind

Scripture teaches that our words can do harm or good. "*The words of the reckless pierce like swords, but the tongue of the wise brings healing*" (**Proverbs 12:18**). When explaining essential changes to your relationship to in-laws and family, choose kind words, but be direct and clear. Ensure everyone understands the need for and the benefit of having appropriate boundaries. You are not cutting family out. Instead, you are building better relationships.

"*The one who has knowledge uses words with restraint, and whoever has understanding is even tempered.*" (**Proverbs 17:27**)

Re-evaluate and Reaffirm Your Boundaries

Situations may arise where you must re-evaluate or reaffirm your boundaries. The arrival of children requires discussing child-rearing and assuring in-laws and family adhere to your parenting choices. And sometimes we all need a refresher on the details. Reaffirming your boundaries shows they remain important because you desire a healthy, happy relationship between you and your spouse and your in-laws and family.

Growing as a family has enough challenges for both newlyweds and those in a well-lived marriage. Starting where you are and working to build better boundaries with in-laws and family, allows you to focus on what matters instead of on what makes matters worse.

Part Four

The Call to Ministry

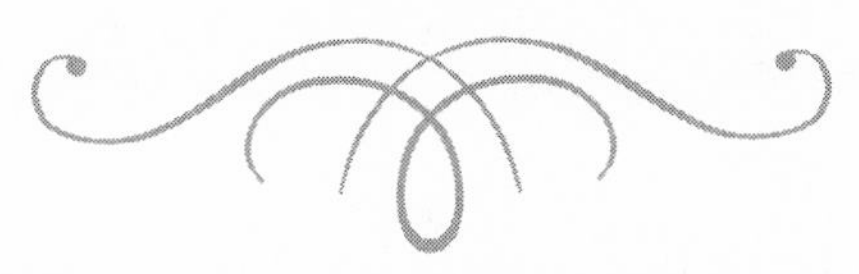

Lee and Darlene Constant

A Christ Center Marriage

I know, I know. When you hear the term, "A Christian Marriage" it sounds trite, cliché and hardly seems to mean anything these days, especially when the divorce rate in the church is just as high with those who aren't confessing Christians.

Despite divorce statistics, it doesn't negate God's word, that He honors marriage (*Hebrews* 13:4). As people, *we* fall short, God's word, never falls short.

When Lee and I first met, I had *(and still do)* a personal relationship with Jesus. Lee did not. This did not discourage me from dating him, because he was a good man, he respected and honored me from day one.

He never mocked me about my faith or going to church, and I never pressured or gave him any ultimatums about attending church or harped on him how he needed to surrender his life to Jesus.

Here's the thing.

I never believed in scare tactics, manipulation, or brow beating someone over the head about attending church or surrendering their life to Jesus. Accepting Jesus Christ, is a personal decision and it should be based on the person's heart, and their personal encounter with Jesus Christ. No one should ever accept Jesus Christ out of fear, coercion, or feel pressured from other people in the church.

The truth is, even though Lee wasn't saved, didn't mean he was an evil man. Everyone who hasn't sought the Lord as their personal Savior isn't vile, evil and demonic like many church people would have you believe. I've experienced evil from people who profess living a life for Jesus Christ, much more than those who did not. With that being said, I've witnessed "saved" couples in the church who not only got divorced, but have remarried two and three times. So, how do two people who profess a life in Christ get divorce? We're they unequally yoke? I'm not telling women to be unequally yoked in their union. What I am saying, it wasn't my story.

If your husband currently isn't saved, he shouldn't get saved or go to church just for you. If he does, it's not going to last, will breed resentment and it will not be real. Accepting Jesus Christ and dedicating one's life to Him, needs to be real to for that person, and shouldn't have anything to do with you. Are you his God?

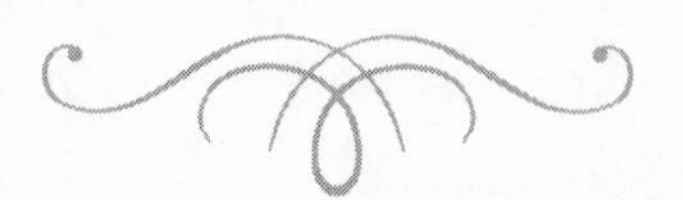

Growing up, I would hear the horror stories from wives who married unsaved men, and experienced all kinds of heartache from infidelity, domestic violence, all kinds of disrespect, etc., from their husbands, and would then blame their husband's behavior on the "Devil" because he had not surrendered their lives to Jesus Christ. However, when their husbands finally surrendered his life to Jesus Christ, the husbands started "acting right" and "treating them right."

Okay, let's take a moment.

A couple of things. Being a critical thinker, I'm always asking "The Why?" Why would it actually take a man to surrender his life to Jesus Christ to treat his wife correctly?

You mean to tell me a husband doesn't know he shouldn't be committing adultery, domestic violence, disrespecting, lying, cheating, etc..., on his wife because he doesn't know Jesus? And the wives who are married to these men believe this is acceptable behavior?

Whewww Chileeee.

Listen, a husband does not need salvation to know right from wrong. We're all born with a conscious, way before we understand the concept of Jesus and Salvation. We all know it's wrong to abuse, cheat, lie, steal, and be disrespectful. A husband (or any person for that matter) doesn't need to be saved, to know how to treat his wife right or any other person.

Sorry to disappoint, but I don't have any horror stories of Lee mistreating me, acting crazy, beating, cursing, disrespecting, or cheating on me, before he surrendered his life to Jesus Christ.

Nope, not our story.

Another why question? How was it Lee, a man who didn't grow up in the church, was even in my purview and not a man from church?

Looking back on my church experience, growing up with the young men in the church who I'd known all my life, should have been great prospects for having a Christ centered marriage when we became adults. Unfortunately, they did not want to be married. Their intentions and desires toward me, was simply to see who would be the first to "bust a nut" inside of me and have bragging rights.

Too much?

Well, if a man who professes being a "Man of God," but only wants to have sex with you, and have no intentions of having the honor of making you his wife, building a godly marriage, what else do you call it?

At the time, I was disappointed, because how could we all be raised in the same church, professed Jesus as our Lord Savior, heard the same messages being preached, but as men, they didn't want to wait for marriage to have sex?

In my book, "It Might Just Be You," I address and describe this acceptable pattern of behavior by men in the church as the "Whorish Double Standard" in the Body of Christ. Women are taught to keep their legs closed, remain pure, or at least have a "low body" count and men are given a pass to run roughshod with their penis into any and every woman who will receive them, without any immediate consequences.

It's hypocritical teaching and Pastoring.

So, although the young men and I were raised in church together, there were clearly two different messages being presented.

Despite being raised in an Atheist household, *(Lee's parents were divorced and his mother did not believe in God)* Lee believed in God for himself. Even before he yielded his life to Christ, he was operating in his spiritual gifts of discernment, prophecy and healing, but at the time he didn't understand it.

Before Lee was saved, the Lord would show me how He was going to use Lee in a powerful way in the Kingdom. He showed me Lee was going to be a Pastor, and not a hireling, but a Pastor after His own heart, having a heart for God's people. Lee would not be bastard son in the pulpit. The Lord spoke this to me, seven years before Lee was ordained and licensed as a Pastor.

I've always prayed for Lee, but as the Lord continued revealing things to me, I shifted my prayers, asking the Lord to cover him, to reach him as only God could, so Lee could begin to establish his own personal relationship with God. Then I began to thank God in advance for the manifestation of His word concerning Lee. Please know, when I prayed for my husband, *(he didn't know I was praying for him)* this did not include me bashing him with scriptures, running around the house speaking in tongues, standing up on Sunday morning asking the 'Saints' to pray for him, going to women's group asking for prayer or even going to the church Pastor.

"I'd rather see a sermon than hear one any day"
~ EDGAR A. GUEST

I've always been of the mindset to cut out the "middle man" and sit before the Lord for myself.

I never once spoke a single scripture to Lee. I never yelled, shouted, screamed, emasculated, shamed or demanded he "Come to church and get saved." That's what silly immature wives do.

I simply lived a Godly life before Lee.

**(Lee did surrender his life to Christ. In his own words, he speaks of his transformation in further detail in chapter "I am My Beloved's")*

Pastor D. Lee Constant

A Pastor's Heart

"...and I will give you Pastor's according to mine heart, which shall feed you with knowledge and understanding"
~Jeremiah 3:15

When Lee surrendered his life to Jesus Christ, it was beautiful and amazing to watch his relationship with God grow. I've always admired Lee's character, his commitment, loyalty, and unwavering obedient mindset to God! Once he said yes to Jesus Christ that was it!

Many times, when people sincerely surrender their lives to God, they're still tempted by the trappings of the world. For many, the traps can come in the form of unsaved family members, friends or other ungodly influences.

Lee was (and still is) a straight SELL OUT for Jesus Christ! He never went back and forth having a "struggle" with his decision, even though it cost him losing family and friends. He was mocked, his character assassinated, and people he had known for years no longer wanted to be in his presence because they felt he was different. Isn't that what transformation in Jesus looks like? Different?

Lee was sad by the rejection from his family and friends, but he wasn't going to allow them to have a stronghold in his life. His mind was made up and if they had a problem with his transformation, it was their issue not his and he didn't seek their approval to live a Christ filled life.

From the time Lee received salvation, he stayed *(and still does)* living his life intentionally to please God. Even in his mistakes, he's quick to own it *(and not blame the "Devil")* repent, seek God's forgiveness and not repeat the same "mistake" over and over again.

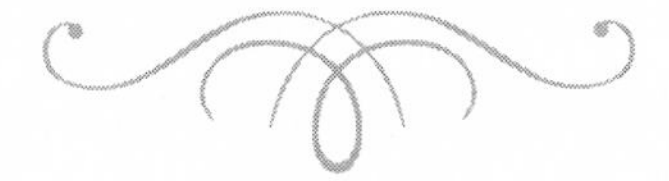

After Lee and I served faithfully for ten years under another ministry, that Pastor recommended Lee to enter into the domination's seminary school. Lee accepted, graduated and was recommended as a candidate for ordination and Pastoral licensing.

During those ten years, I watched Lee grow through his growing pains, as he served with integrity, resilience, strength and power *(because true power, is when you don't seek vengeance on those who treat you like dung.)* Lee's service in ministry reminds me of the scripture, Ephesians 6:7 "*Serve with good will, as to the Lord and not to men.*"

The Lord was preparing him in his growing pains. Lee is truly a Pastor after God's own heart. The Lord continued to bless Lee, as he matured in the ways of the Lord, learning and doing work in the ministry...And the FAVOR that has been on Lee's life, Whewwwww!

Four years after Lee's ordination and licensing ceremony, the Lord called us out to establish the ministry God's House of Restoration (GHR)

As the Pastor of GHR Lee definitely has the heart of God as it relates to feeding, guiding, growing and reconciling the broken-hearted back to God. He truly loves and honors people always wanting the best for them, staying in constant *(pun intended)* prayer before the Lord.

A church is truly blessed when their Pastor has the heart of God. A Pastor who is unwavering, leads with integrity, loves God's people, who walks in compassion and empathy; A Pastor who has a caring heart about people during their good times and during times of turbulence; A Pastor who understands, this isn't about them, it's about souls, reconciling people back to God.

GHR is truly blessed to have Lee as their Pastor. Yes, Lee is my husband, but he's also my Pastor. I tell Lee all the time, "You are the BEST PASTOR, I've ever had and I simply honor and adore you!"

Author and Lady D.C. Constant

A Pastor's Wife

As I previously stated, I had known for years Lee would become a Pastor, and during this time, I had taken issue with the Lord, because again, I did not want to be a Pastor's wife.

For years, my conversations with God would be the same way, "Whelp Lord, this is something I do not want to do, so I guess I'm going to die and Lee's going to get another wife, because I'm not feeling this...I think I told you before, I don't feel like dealing with your "Adult Children."

Yeah. Looking back on those conversations, I was tripping and having my own "adult tantrum!"

It wasn't I didn't feel "qualified" to be a Pastor's wife, we had already been working together for years in ministry and God had truly blessed us to be a blessing to others. The truth was, I didn't want to operate at that level in ministry, due to the unnecessary frustration that comes with dealing with some of God's people and to be frank, in my experience, culturally in mostly (not all) African-American churches, many of the people could be extremely brutal, disrespectful, nasty and downright ugly toward leadership.

Especially toward the Pastor's wife.

It wasn't something that scared me, because Mr. Constant would never allow anyone to disrespect me. I simply didn't want to be bothered with the hypocrisy of it all.

These were the honest on and off again conversations I would have with God for years, until one night during a church revival the Lord DEALT with me!

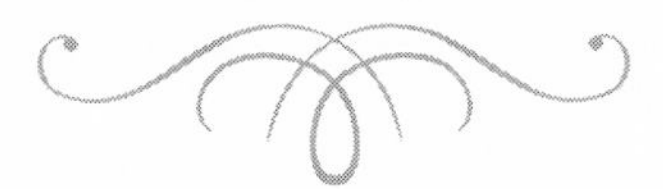

Before we started GHR, God had spoken to Lee for us to start the ministry, I hesitated... no let me use the correct word, I was still being "hard headed," about starting GHR. Lee had spoken to me in great detail about the vision God had shown him, and what the ministry would entail. I was proud of how the Lord was going to use him during this next elevation in ministry, but I wasn't ready to start a church and I shared this with Lee.

There were two realities going on within me.

On this one particular evening, we were at home getting ready to attend a church revival service and I brought up again about not wanting to start a church.

Me: "Babe, I don't think we need to start a church. I think we should just leave where we are, go assist in another person's ministry, stay there for a few years, and then start the ministry the Lord has for us."

Lee: He was quite for a moment, he then looked me dead in my eyes and said, "Darlene, that is not what the Lord is telling me to do."

Let me tell you something about Pastor Constant, when it comes to obeying what the Lord has told him to do, He's going to obey God! No matter who you are, and it doesn't matter if you can see the vision or not, or disagree with him. Even if it's me, He's going to obey God!

Me: "I know, but...*(This conjunction right here, let's you know I was definitely having a "silly woman" moment.)* I feel we should just go to another church and assist them.

As we continued to get dress, I kept rattling off the list of reasons why I didn't want to start the ministry, which God had clearly instructed us to do. Lee never said another word.

Now where in the car, headed to the church revival, and I'm still "running my mouth." Lee was quiet the whole ride to church. You know why?

Because "He said, what he said."

When we arrived at the church revival, just walking through the doors, you could feel God's anointing and presence in the atmosphere. The revival was being led by Evangelist Doris Ellison, a true Prophet, a mighty preacher and warrior in the God's Kingdom. What I love and respect about Evangelist Ellison, is she doesn't play when it comes to God's word or His people, but most importantly she lives the life she preaches about! She has a pure heart and passion for God's people and she's going to tell you the truth in love, whether you like it or not.

During this period in my life, when I needed a mother figure, Evangelist Ellison was the only woman who I saw as such, after I vowed I never would never look at any one in ministry like that again. Evangelist Ellison, wasn't like any of the others. The Lord placed her in my life because she was proven to be trust worthy, never taking sides, and has still been a "constant" force in my life. She has watched me grow in the ministry for over twenty plus years, and has still proven to be a trusted confidante.

How God was moving in the revival service was nothing short of AWESOME! When Evangelist Ellison was done preaching she made an altar call. To give context for those who may not know, an altar call is when a Preacher ask those in the congregation to freely come to the altar for prayer, deliverance, or for any need they may have and pray for them. On occasion, the Preacher may look at someone from the congregation and ask them to come to the altar.

I remember this moment like it was yesterday. I was standing, clapping and rejoicing in the Lord, when Evangelist Ellison made eye contact with me and motioned for me to come to the alter. As I walked down the aisle to the altar, "I wondered, what is this about? I don't have any prayer request, I'm good?

Unlike most prophets who shame and embarrass people by speaking their business out loud when they're at the altar, Evangelist Ellison, did not put me on "blast." She leaned over, and whispered in my ear: "God said, SHUT UP! SHUT YOUR MOUTH! You will not go to another ministry to assist anyone, that is not what He has instructed you to do! You will do what He has called you to do! Stop trying to influence your husband about this! God has already given the instruction and direction about the ministry He has called you both too! SHUT YOUR MOUTH!

All I remember after receiving that word, was getting up off the floor, (*I had fell out, and was slain in the spirit*) and church service was over. I was still crying when I walked up to Lee and said, "So when are we leaving this church, and starting the ministry?" The Lord never had to deal with me on that level ever again when it came to ministry. I had it coming though. I mean, for years, I kept telling the Lord want I didn't want to do, and yes He was gracious to listen, then he got tired of my whining and said, "Okay, enough! Shut up and go do what I've called you to do."

Listen, Evangelist Ellison, had no idea the conversation Lee and I had just discussed before arrival at the revival, and I had never shared with her the vision God had given us about starting a ministry.

The next day while in prayer I began to speak to the Lord. This was the exact conversation:

"Hi Lord, I hope you're doing well today and I haven't grieved you in anyway. Lord I repent for my attitude and about not wanting to do what you've called me to do and I thank you for the chastisement at the revival. So, since this is happening, I would like to make a specific request regarding women in the ministry. You know the betrayal and pain I've experienced with women in ministry whom I thought loved me, only to learn of the jealousy, and envy they felt toward me. Lord, I honestly don't have time for those type of shenanigans in the ministry you're entrusting to us with.

I would like to request the type of women I'd like to work with who you will be sending top work with me in this ministry you've entrusted Lee and I with. You know I don't do gossip, so I need them to be seasoned mature women, who are able to assist and guide other women who aren't seasoned without judgment. I need women who can work with me and not against me; I need women who will not shun, other women whom they feel who don't act a certain way, dress in what they feel is inappropriate, or whom they don't deem "worthy" of salvation. I need women who will love on your people and honestly get to know them, and seek you on their behalf on how to help them. I need women who can agree and disagree respectfully, and we can still break bread together. I need married women who are happy in you and in their marriages. I need single women who are happy in you, and aren't messy and will wait on your guidance and direction for a husband. Without question, I need your wisdom and guidance when ministering to your people. Especially women, because I don't play! I need to be restored from the pain other women have caused me, so I don't bleed and hurt the women you will send this ministry.

In Jesus Name, Amen."

As I laid there, the Holy Spirit spoke to my heart and said two words. "BE IT."

I wasn't the quickest deer in the forest, I keep repeating, "Be It?" "Be It" "Be...." Ohhhhhh okay Lord, everything, I just prayed how I want the women to be, I need to "Be It!" Lead by example! Okay, Got It!

That was over fifteen years ago.

I recently spoke with Evangelist Ellison and recalled with her the night of the church revival. She gasp and said, "I don't remember saying that! WOW, that could have moved you right into being offended"

I told her it didn't offend me, because I knew what she had told me had come straight from God, because she had absolutely no idea what I had just spoken to Lee before we had arrived at the revival, and it was for me to remember, not her. I told her, "I can laugh about it now, because I use it as a teaching tool when I'm ministering to others."

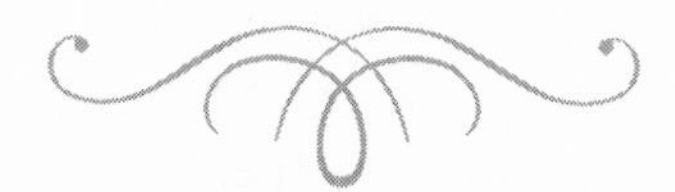

For me, being a Pastor's Wife is a blessing, as Lee and I always have each other's back. I keep him covered in prayer, and I don't have identity any issues about knowing who I am in Christ's Kingdom. I have many gifts and talents I contribute to God's House of Restoration, as I'm a Co-laborer in the ministry with Lee and I'm not the Pastor.

As the Pastor's wife, make sure to be yourself, know who you are in Christ, because if you don't, others will smell it on you and try to give you their definition what a Pastor's Wife should and should not be. You'll end up utterly confused, resentful and bitter, trying to live up to a false expectation of pleasing people. This definitely isn't my testimony, but in my church experience, I've seen this happen many times to Pastor's wives.

You may have heard the saying, "Be his peace." This is especially true being a wife, with a husband in ministry. As much as it's rewarding leading God's people, it's also difficult and hard, especially when you're doing it God's way, and not for selfish reasons. There are many statistics about Pastors feeling lonely, depressed, frustrated, having no authentic friendships, and not having an outlet for their pain, etc., Although this varies from Pastor to Pastor, it's important to make sure you're covering him in prayer, have peace in your home and have enough self-awareness to know when the enemy is trying to use YOU to get to your husband.

Allow your husband to be himself. Don't compare or expect him to be like any other Pastor. He isn't. Your husband is the Pastor whom God has designed him to be for the congregation He's entrusted you both with. Be blessed by them and never compare your ministry to anyone else's.

Please know, there's a certain way you must carry yourself being the wife of a Pastor, Deacon, Minister, etc.., This doesn't mean you need to be fake/phony, or trying to be someone you're not, or feeling you need to change your whole personality. This has more to do with exercising decorum in the face of obstacles, and other people's foolishness, and not having a wayward spirit, because you do represent your husband and people are watching you.

It comes with the territory. Don't take it personally.

Most importantly, next to God, make sure your husband doesn't feel he's doing ministry alone. You guys are a team!

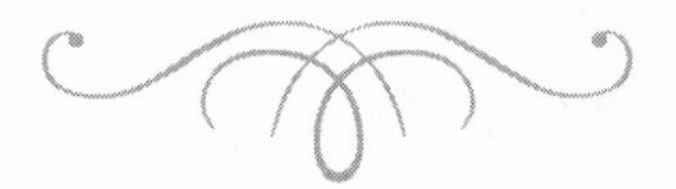

As a Pastor's Wife, I often get questions from other Pastor's wives how to deal with disrespectful women, when it comes to their husband. Honestly, that's a marital discussion you need to have with your husband. You both should be able have transparent conversations about any men or women in the church who approach either of you inappropriately, by taking preventive measures, setting boundaries between the clergy and the congregation, while having steps in place to handle inappropriate situations should it arise.

For me, becoming a Pastor's wife, didn't make me feel apprehensive about dealing with women in the church. It wasn't even on my radar, because I've never had any issues with Lee dishonoring me when it came to women before he was a Pastor, so why be concerned about it now?

Now, of course, I knew women who wanted to sleep with Lee (*before and after he became a Pastor*) however, for me it's never about any woman, but it's about the actions of my husband (*or for any wife's husband*) that determines what "goes" or doesn't "go down." Having honest conversations about the opposite sex is something Lee and I have been doing since the beginning of our relationship. For us, it's a no brianer.

I'll share with you three situations where I've experienced rude women and how I handled them in the Godliest manner I possible could at the time. I'm not saying this is how every Pastor's wife or any woman of God should handle these situations, I'm sharing to bring awareness how the enemy will show up anywhere and will use anybody to bring division, test your faith and try to "seduce" you out your Godly character.

Even when righteous anger is justifiable.

#True Story

The year Lee was ordained and licensed as a Pastor; it was at a church convention. During a break in the service, I went to use the restroom. A woman who was a well-known Evangelist, single, was known to be on the "prowl" desperately wanting to be a Pastor's Wife, walked in and came right up to me. I was standing at the sink, washing my hands, and she began to inquire if I were the wife of the newly ordained Pastor Constant. When I confirmed I was, she began to speak very LOUDLY sounding "intimidating."

Evangelist: "Oh okay," she said, with hand movements. "Listen, you a Passata's wife now, and you better watch out for those women coming after your husband! He's a fineeeee young man!"

Me: "Yes he is. Thank you."

Evangelist: "How long ya'll been married?"

Me: "Fourteen years."

Evangelist: "Oh yeah, that's good, that's really good."

She proceeded to continue with unsolicited advice telling me how and what type of Pastor's Wife I needed to be...I kept washing my hands, which at this point were cleaner than a baby's bottom.

When she finished talking, I asked, "Are you done?"

Evangelist: "Oh, yes."

Me: "Let me ask you a question."

Evangelist: Looked perplex.

Me: "You know when you go on a job interview, you ace it and the hiring manager offers you the job, and they also give you the job description and not your soon to be co-workers?"

Evangelist: Didn't answer, but still looking perplex.

Me: "Well, God is my hiring manager and He'll give me my job description and will guide me how to assist my husband in leading His (God) people in the role He's prepared for me. Also, I'm the Pastor's wife, I'm not the congregation's wife."

Her: She kept silent, gave me a dirty look, and then left.

I finally dried my hands, and as I walked out the door, I said, "God, you do realize all kinds of crazy stuff has happened to me in the bathroom right? Sheeshhh"

Now, keep in mind, this Evangelist did not personally know me or my husband. She was just loud and wrong. A combination which doesn't work well for me when I'm being approached in that manner.

Everyone wants to tell Pastor's Wives to look out for other women in the church. Trust me, we already know, and the truth is they can't stop any woman from wanting to sleep with their husband. Whether your husband is a Pastor or not, it's his responsibility to protect you and shut down the foolishness from other women, before it becomes a problem.

I've sat in many women's ministry groups where they would tell women to pray and ask God not allow their husbands to commit adultery. Me being me, you know, a free thinker, I would object to participating in those types of prayer, as I found them to be based in fear and rooted in insecurities. I had been married for years, and it never crossed my mind to ask God to make sure Lee "kept it" in his pants. Do men's ministry groups sit around teaching this and praying to God, asking Him to make sure their wives don't cheat?

I highly doubt it.

God gives everyone free will *(even wives)* and the bottom line is this: Every husband knows where his "stick" belongs and he makes the final decision where he will and will not "poke it."

Plus, I'm not nor have I ever been a penis babysitter.

#True Story

About twenty-years ago, I worked at the headquarters for a giant retail company and the department I worked in at the time, were comprised of eighty percent women, with most openly professing their faith as Christians. They would discuss church activities, recite biblical scriptures, and throw in the latest dudes they were having sexual relations with.

One morning, after six months of being in this department, I did something I had never done previously on any job. I brought a picture to work that had Lee and Amber-Lee on it, and I was placing it on my desk, when my coworker at the time, "Lydia," walked pass and with excitement grab the picture from my hand and said, "Ohhhhhh is this your husband?"

Me: "Yes."

Lydia: "Ohhhhhh Darlene you've been holding out! Girllll, he's FINEEEEE! Girl I will FUCK HIM AND FUCK HIM WELL!"

Now, Lydia was one of the professing saved "Woman of God" who talked about scriptures, the different men she had slept with, and how she sang and directed her church choir and was a part of a gospel traveling choir made up of various women from different churches in the city.

Me: I just stared at her. I tend to do this a lot when people say or do something inappropriate.

She began walking around to the various cubicles showing the other Christian women my picture. She was loud and proud, as she shouted, "Hey ya'll, Darlene been holding out! Ya'll come see this picture of her husband."

Me: I thought to myself, Wow! No mention of Amber-Lee huh? I mean she's in the picture too.

A circle of women formed around her and began looking at the picture, and Lydia kept repeating to them how she would sleep with my husband and what she would do to him.

She finally made her way back to my cubicle and handed me my picture.

Me: I placed the picture on my desk and said, "You know Lydia, I can appreciate you telling me up front what your intentions are, because in my experience dealing with women, they usually try to befriend me first, before they try to get into bed with my husband."

I then extended my hands and asked her, "Would you like to pray now?"

Lydia: Her eyes got wide and she screamed, "BITCH THAT'S WHY I HATE YOU! I REALLY HATE YOU!"

Me: "Soooooo, that's a no on the prayer?"

She walked away and went back to her cubicle.

#True Story

Many years ago, a single woman joined the ministry where Lee and I served and over a two-year period of her being a member of the church, she wasted no time flirting and sleeping with most of the singled and married in the church. It had gotten to the point of being so disruptive and chaotic, many of the wives wanted to physically "lay hands" on her and I don't mean in a prayerful way.

This wasn't a "rumor" or folks gossiping about her sleeping around, because she openly admitted to anyone who would listen to her about her sexual escapades. After two years, she decided to move on and leave the church, but before she left, she came to talk with me.

Her: "Sis. Constant, I just want to let you know, you have a good husband, because I tried everything I could to make him pay me some attention and he never did."

Me: "Sis, really? Was he supposed to have paid you some attention?"

Her: "Yeah he was, because I've never met a man who didn't pay me any attention and didn't want to sleep with me. I tried hard to get at your husband, but he and the Pastor were the only two I couldn't get too. The rest of the men were easy."

Me: Orrr..... maybe you were just easy?

Her: Whatever Sis. Constant, she said laughing as she walked away.

Here's the thing.

Prior to her approaching me, Lee and I had already discussed and "peep her game." We knew what she was about, and he had already told me about her advances. She thought because I never approached her, I didn't know what was going on. I didn't need to say anything to her, because Lee had already handled it.

"Cherish and Enjoy each
chapter of your lives together"

Enjoying your Wifehood Journey

You can have as much fun in your marriage as you determine to have. You do know, God did not put you together to be miserable right?

He didn't put you together to fight, pick on each other or try to change each other. The Bible says, "*That a woman is to enjoy her husband*" (1 Peter 3:2 AMPC)

Your wifehood journey is what you make of it. You will define what enjoyment you get and feel from being your husband's wife.

No big secret there.

You can listen, glean, and watch other people's marriages, but how you and your husband envision and live out that vision in your marriage will be solely based on the two of you.

I embrace and enjoy my wifehood journey through all its seasons. I'm a Kingdom wife, with a Kingdom marriage whose desire is to please God. I understand my God given assignment is to be my husband's *helpmate* and not his *headache.*

Next to God, nothing comes before me being a wife. My marriage is my first ministry. I'm intentional with prioritizing my time in prayer, covering my husband, the ministry, and sowing good seed on fertile ground within our marriage, by staying at the feet of Jesus, seeking His counsel on all things. I do not accept any outside commitments not adding value to my marriage or will make me stagnant as a wife.

We never put our child before our marriage. This may be difficult for some wives and especially single women with children who are looking to be married one day, to hear this type of message. The marriage comes before the children. This doesn't mean you're putting a man before your children; it means, your children need to see a unity in your union; A marriage where two people are loving and committed to one another, providing them with stability, safety and security.

Understand, your role as wife and mother are two very distinctive roles. You're a wife to your husband and a mother to the children, and whether the children are biological or stepchildren neither should be "running" your marriage.

I'm intentional every day, (*even in making my mistakes*) cultivating a Godly marriage pleasing unto the Lord. Most importantly, I have FUN and act GOOFY with my husband!

We have our own marital language, intertwined and extremely close.

Issac Kubvoruno puts it this way, "A *virtuous wife treats her husband in a way that affirms his manhood, emboldens his spiritual leadership, in a manner that causes him to rejoice that she is his wife. Every woman can be a wife, but it takes divine wisdom, courage, and strength to be a virtuous wife. Do not just be a wife. Be a virtuous wife. 'A virtuous woman who can find? For her price is far above rubies*" ~Proverbs 31:10

How are you enjoying your wifehood journey?

____

____

____

____

____

____

____

____

____

____

____

____

____

____

____

____

____

____

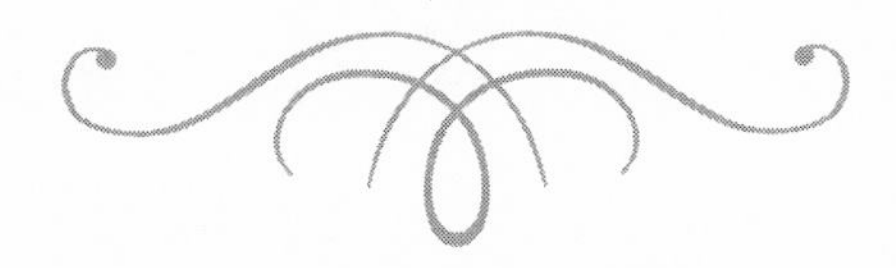

Part Five

Keep the "Sexy" in Sex

After 30 years, with 25 years being married, not only do we still walk in love together, but most importantly, we continue laughing together and at each other...

What's Your Sex Language?

"Marriage is to be held in honor among all, and the marriage bed is undefiled" ~Hebrews 13:4

God created sex and it's a beautiful within the confines of marriage, as the marriage bed is honorable and undefiled. *Hebrews* 13:4. Meaning in God's eyes, it isn't corrupt, impure, untainted or unclean.

As a wife, you should never allow anyone to make you feel ashamed for loving and enjoying having sex with your husband.

In 1Corinthians 7:9 Paul admonishes the unmarried to get married, because they were burning with passion for one another. Passion in the Greek, means "to set on fire."

Sex sets us on fire and God says the place for it, is in the marital bed. So, wives enjoy every bit of your sex life and take joy setting your husband on "fire" with your passion!

It's God's plan.

I believe if married couples would have honest ongoing conversations about sex sharing their likes/ dislikes, instead of viewing sex from a worldly perverse perspective, there wouldn't be as many adulterous affairs taking place within the Body of Christ.

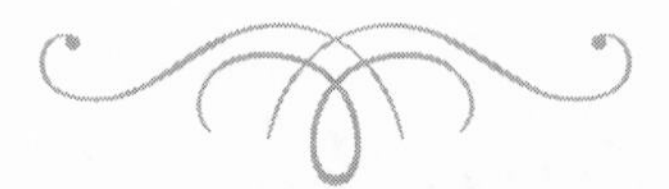

Many are familiar with Dr. Gary Chapman, author of the book The Five Love Languages. According to Chapman, our "love language" described below, is how we receive love from others.

Words of Affirmation. Saying supportive things to your partner.

Acts of Service - Doing helpful things for your partner

Receiving Gifts - Giving your partner gifts that tell them you we're thinking about them

Quality Time - Spending meaningful time with your partner

Physical Touch - Being close to and caressed by your partner

However, what about our sex languages? Did you even know you had a sex language? Do you know what's your Sex Language? Do you know your partner's Sex Language?

Psychologist and author Douglas Weiss Ph.D. shares an overview of the five different sex languages we possess and how you have the keys to open the doors to sexual pleasure for your partner and from your partner.

Let's go through the five sex languages briefly here.

Sex Language 1: Fun

The fun sex language person's pleasure is accentuated when you mix fun with sex. This person is going to enjoy spontaneity, various locations, and creativity during all phases of sex.

Sex Language 2: Desire

The desire sex language person's sexuality is heightened if they feel pursued and wanted. They love you planning their sexual time and encounter. Their pleasure is you really wanting them sexually.

Sex Language 3: Pleasure

If your partner's sex language is pleasure, they will want to learn how to please you. They want to experiment as to what gives the most pleasure during a sex act. Their exploring and being explored takes sex to another level for this person.

Sex Language 4: Patience

Slow it down. Take your time. And a lot of time, are some of the mantras of the patience sex language. This person enjoys massages and gentleness before, during and after sex.

Sex Language 5:Acceptance/Celebration

The person who has an acceptance/celebration sex language wants to know you accept and celebrate all who they are. During every phase of sex, they want you to appreciate all they are to you, not just their body or sexually. Being valued makes sex more satisfying for this person.

No matter how long you've been married or what sexual season your marriage is currently in, understand sex is a vital component. Just as "The Five Love Languages," illustrates the importance of understanding your spouse love language, your spouse sex language is just as important.

Part Six

The Conclusion of the Whole Matter

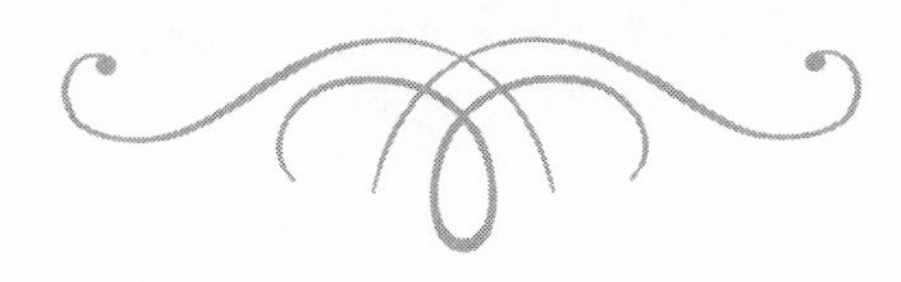

"I am My Beloved's and My Beloved is Mine"
~Song of Solomon

I AM MY BELOVED'S

By: D. Lee Constant

Our Editorial Director, Elizabeth Rattray, sat down with Lee Constant, husband of Darlene "D.C". Constant, for a chat to share his perspective about Darlene and his views on having and maintaining a healthy marriage.

Describe your thoughts when you first saw Darlene?

When I first saw Darlene, I was like damn who is that? She had on this nice green dress that caught my eyes and that's all I saw. Everything else around me was nonexistent.

I quickly recognized her intelligence and wittiness. I also found her sexy. She was also uppity. She thought and acted like I wasn't on her level intellectually. She didn't think I picked up on it, but I did and got those digits anyway and the rest as they say is history.

When did you know Darlene was "The One" for you? Was it something she said or did? How was she different from any other woman you've experienced?

Darlene was definitely different and not like any woman I've ever met. It was something about her. She was refreshingly honest *(she still is)* and all I knew was I wanted this thing we had to keep going.

We would meet every day for lunch at this little Italian restaurant, and Darlene didn't eat Italian, but loved the ambiance. We would just order beverages, talking getting to know each other, until we got kicked out and was told not to come back to the restaurant because we weren't spending any money. We kept meeting for lunch, but started taking walks. The more time we spent together the more I fell for her.

Now, Darlene's plan for me was only being the 'fun guy' in her life, and nothing more. Even though I had already fallen for her, *(she didn't know this)* I purposed in my heart not to care that she looked at me in this way, because I thought after the summer, whatever this was would be over.

Describe what you thought about her belief in God, even though you weren't raised in the church?

Darlene was saved *(had accepted salvation)* and went to church. I wasn't saved nor did I attend church and Darlene going to church wasn't a big deal to me. I was fine with it. When I was younger, my dad took me to church so it wasn't like I didn't understand it. I was cool with it. Her belief system didn't scare me away.

Describe you and Darlene's dating journey.

Pre-Darlene, my dating journey was simple. No long-term commitments, no attachments and when the women would drop the "L" word, *you know Love*, I just disappeared. All my 'relationships' were based on sex and they all FAILED.

All my life, I would hear people talk about how relationships should have a foundation not based on sex first. I thought to myself how I would give it a shot. To actually get to know a woman first, before having sex with her. Enter, Darlene... literally the next woman I met after making this declaration to myself.

Our foundation was built on honesty. Brutal at times, but refreshing. One thing about Darlene, she articulated how she felt and she wasn't for any B.S. I was in love with this woman. She definitely came up on my blind slide.

Our foundation was built on solid ground. We didn't have sex for months and that was ok with me. It was different and refreshing, because I was used to woman giving it up really easy. Actually, I wasn't looking for that *(not that I didn't want her sexually)*, but I had purposed in my mind that wanted to have something more from a relationship with a woman, besides her spreading opening her legs, and Darlene wasn't that type of woman.

Our journey has had its highs and lows, ups and downs. Through it all, there was no one else *(still isn't)* I wanted to be with. We laughed, cried, had and continue to have so much fun together.

Describe your feelings during her journey with therapy sessions? How did this affect you emotionally How did you view Darlene while going through it?

I was angry, heartbroken, dumbfounded and just plain pissed about what Darlene had gone through, which was beyond unnecessary. I know we all go through things in our childhood, but damn I would have never accepted that. I often tell Darlene, had I grown up in church and experienced what she did, I can honestly say, I wouldn't be in church now. During this time, I was amazed how she never blamed or hated God and how today she's a big advocate for black men.

I attended some of Darlene's therapy sessions, so that I could get a better understanding of what she was going through so I could help her in some form or fashion. As the sessions went on I knew that resentment was coming my way because I was the closest man to her and even though it was done unintentionally it hurt like nothing I had ever felt before.

I saw Darlene's vulnerability that made me appreciate her in unimaginable ways. I gained a better under-standing of why she directed her angry toward me. As she worked through therapy, she did work hard and did the best she knew how to apply the tools her therapist recommended. When she confronted her stepfather, I was proud of her! That was courageous. Darlene simply intrigues me.

Describe how you feel about Darlene being your wife and your marriage journey?

I'm honored that Darlene is my wife. I love her like I've never loved any other woman. I love how she and I continue to walk in love. My journey has been an adventure with her. Honesty, never boring or a dull moment.

In our nearly 26 years of marriage and 30yrs of being together, we've experienced a multitude of situations and circumstances, but through it all we always had each other's back. She has always been in the fox hole with me. Trying to mesh two worlds into one, without losing yourself is challenging, but we did it. We became one without losing who we are individually. She's my ride or die.

How did you view being a "boyfriend" vs. being a husband?"

Initially my view was, they're both the same thing. I was committed, so what was the big deal? As our journey continued, I realized marriage was the difference between a boy and a man.

Marriage tells your spouse and the world simultaneously this woman is worth all of me for as long as God gives me breath. I wanted to provide, protect, raise a family and live my best life with one woman and she was beyond worth it. I'm glad I grew up.. Lol

What has marriage taught you about yourself?

Marriage has taught me not be selfish, to grow and mature. Marriage will define you one way or another. It has challenged me to finish what I start and to keep my word to my wife at all times.

What's one of your favorite funny stories of you and Darlene?

Oh Wow! There are sooooooo many funny ones, but one of the funniest was back in the summer of 1993. I was still living with my mom, and had the entire third floor to myself. Darlene and I were playing around wrestling on the bed like we've done plenty of times. But on this particular day, we were playing really crazy.

We were laughing, pillow fighting, talking smack, rough-housing, tackling and tickling each other, while wrestling on the bed which was about 5 feet from the wall-- and the next thing we knew, we went right through it! Yes. The wall!

There was this long pause.... we looked at each other with our eyes bucked like, oh sh—! What the hell just happened? Then we burst into laughter so hard until our stomach hurt and was crying real tears! I'm so glad it was dry wall.

My sister Karey heard the loud noise and came upstairs walking in my room and her mouth dropped when she saw the large hole in the wall. She then looked at us. "So, what the hell was y'all doing?" she asked. At the same time Darlene and I started shaking our head, and still laughing, saying, "No, no, no, Karey it's not what you think. Really." She started laughing and of course she didn't believe us, but she never told moms on us either.

Darlene had an Uncle who was a carpenter whom she called and explained what happened. He came the same day with his tools. He took one looked at the wall, looked at us, studying the hole, then said, "Ya'll was just rough housing, playing huh? Yeah okay."

Darlene and I just started and couldn't stop laughing. We promised him we weren't "getting busy." He didn't believe us. After he fixed the wall, by replastering it, you couldn't tell two bodies had just gone through it.

What was one of the most challenging situations you've encountered in your marriage?

The most challenging situation we encountered was when we went to counseling. All marriages go through rough patches and it's those times when a third party is needed to help each spouse understand one another.

The counseling sessions revealed to me areas where I needed improvement which helped my marriage continue to succeed. I'm glad to say our marriage is even greater today because we sought out counseling and it revealed areas were we both needed to develop. I'm proud to say we both did the work and we're continuing to grow.

There are wives whose husbands aren't saved. Describe how Darlene treated you before you knew life with Jesus?

When I met Darlene, she was saved and I wasn't and she didn't treat me differently because I wasn't.

When she would go to church services and come back home, she never made me feel resentful toward her. She never used phrases like "The Pastor was preaching about you today" "You're the Devil" "You need Jesus" "When you gone get saved?" She also wasn't telling me how I needed to be like the Pastor or any other brother in the church.

She never gossiped, talked bad about the church or the people. I would see how joyful she was when she'd get home and I would ask her about it and she would be all pump and excited telling me about the Pastor's sermon, but I didn't fully understand what she was talking about. Yet, it didn't stop me from asking her.

Darlene was a living witness to me of salvation. She never pressured, guilt tripped, placed ultimatums, or "beat" me over the head with scriptures. As a matter of fact, she never quoted any scriptures to me. She literately lived the life of Jesus Christ before me. She would always say, when a person decides to surrender their life to Christ, it should never be for someone else. It's a personal decision.

So, December 1998 rolls around and Darlene was going to a night watch service (a time set aside for corporate intercessory prayer). I was supposed to drop her off and come back to pick her up. I thought I was going over to my boy's house to get high. But that didn't happen.

When I would drop Darlene off, I ended up staying for the service. After we got home, Darlene and our one-year-old daughter, Amber- Lee went to sleep. It was around 1 a.m. and I was in the other room smoking pot.

Fifteen to twenty minutes passed, and I clearly heard this voice tell me, "Repent." My response was, "When I'm finish smoking this joint." I heard the voice a second time, "Repent," and again, I said "When I'm finished smoking."

Now, I see my chest expanding before my eyes, which I've never experience before when smoking weed, yet I still didn't repent. I heard the voice for the third time, "Repent." This time, I took heed and experienced a change of heart that resulted in a turning away from sin. I flushed the joint I was smoking, and went and got my stash and flushed it all down the toilet. I gave my life to Jesus Christ the Son of God, right then and there in my bathroom and I haven't looked back since. That was over twenty-four years ago.

As a husband and Pastor, how do you balance pro- tecting your wife? Does protection look different being a husband vs. a Pastor?

Protecting your spouse as a Husband/Pastor looks the same. Protection in my marriage means no one will step to her in a disrespectful manner, and providing a safe home environment for my family.

It's very important for the husband to protect his wife because she is looking for the peace of mind knowing that whatever happens in the marriage the husband will be there in every capacity needed. Day, night, 365/24-7. I know Darlene can handle herself, I'm her protector not because I think she can't protect herself, I'm her protect because I value her. She's important to me.

As a Pastor the same thing applies. Except in the church, a Pastor must maintain a balance between church and his family. Even though Darlene works side by side with me in the ministry, I still make sure our first ministry, which is our marriage, remains intact. Our marriage and family is our first ministry.

What wisdom can you share in general to wives about their husbands?

I would say to wives, in general, that husbands want the same things you want, at the same level and intensity: To be loved, respected, encouraged, supported, appreciated, and understood.

Most importantly, listen to your husband when he's talking and take him seriously. Do not listen to respond, argue, or to tear him down. Listen to understand his heart and to resolve the issue at hand.

Lee and Darlene playing around

BEFORE YOU SAY "I DO"

For most single women, before they get married they have list... A long list of what they want in a potential husband. I had a pretty long list. The list contains the usual suspects, money, car, his own home, educated, preferably no kids, clean cut, a provider, protector, God fearing, and can lead the family. Not necessarily in that order, as the order will vary from each woman.

When you're single, people who are married will tend to give you and/or engaged couples advice which includes all their mistakes and horror stories. When I was single, all I heard was, 'Just say no to marriage,' 'Marriage is like a job,' 'All husbands cheat,' and the real bitter women, would say, "Hey if it doesn't work out, just get a divorce."

Here's the thing.

Marriage is what you and your husband will make of it. Period.

For many engaged couples, sex clouds their judgement from having concrete and hard conversations, which are needed before they say, "I Do."

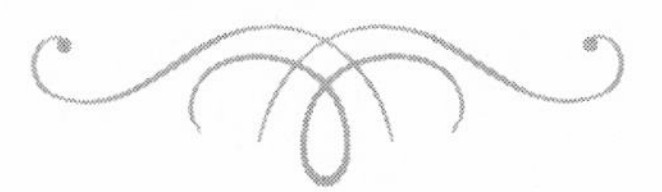

Below are 100 Questions you and your Fiancé should discuss in great detail before getting married.

The importance of these questions is to ensure that you and your partner are on the same page. The most important thing is to keep an open mind, approaching both your own answers and those your partner gives from a place of authentic curiosity, honesty and trust.

Having Children and Starting a Family

Starting a family is one of the most important topics to have covered before you get married. If the two of you aren't on the same page about whether or not to have kids, how to raise them if you want to, and how you feel about things like medical treatment, education and mental health, years down the line you could find yourselves facing deeply serious dilemmas.

1. Do you want to have children?
2. How many?
3. When do you want to start trying?
4. What are you willing to do if we can't have children naturally (IVF treatments, surrogate, egg donation,

sperm donation, adoption)?
5. What if we agree either not to have or to have kids, and I change my mind?
6. What are the most important values you are planning to teach our children?
7. What kind of parenting approach are you planning to implement?
8. What kind of discipline is appropriate or not appropriate?
9. When we start having children, how do you envision your share of responsibilities?
10. What is your perspective on having one of us be a stay-at-home parent?
11. If you or I have children from a previous relationship, how do you envision our blended family?
12. If you have kids from a previous relationship, what role are you willing to take or would like me to take with the step-children?
13. How do you feel about my family?
14. Who is your favorite and least favorite family member on my side and on your side, and why?
15. How often are we going to visit or receive visits from our families?
16. How do you expect to spend the holidays?
17. Do you plan to live near your parents or move near them as they get older?

Intimacy

While a fulfilling sex life is essential to a healthy relationship, intimacy extends beyond sex. Being in sync when it comes to physical pleasure, as well as understanding what each of you need to have your emotional needs met, will bring you both closer, whereas a lack of communication in this area is sure to tear you apart.

18. What are your expectations regarding sex?
19. How open are you to telling me if you are not satisfied sexually?
20. What do you enjoy most about sex?
21. Do you consume pornography and, if so, how do you feel about it?
22. What turns you on most about me?
23. Have you ever had doubts about your sexuality?
24. Do you think I am physically affectionate enough in our relationship?
25. Do you think you can trust me enough to discuss our sexual differences, concerns or fantasies?
26. Is there anything that is off limits sexually?
27. Do you agree to bring up any attraction you are feeling outside of our relationship before something significant develops?

Dealing with Conflict

Marriage is full of ups and downs, and married couples will no doubt get into arguments throughout the course of the relationship. It's how you deal with this conflict that will determine if your relationship has the strength to get through the tough times.

28. What is your conflict response — avoidance, accommodation, compromise, or something else?

29. How did your family deal with conflict growing up?
30. How do you usually express anger?
31. How comfortable are you with having arguments or disagreements?
32. What do you think our perpetual conflicts are (those based in personality or lifestyle differences)?
33. What part of me is most annoying to you?
34. What would be an example of a resolvable conflict in our relationship?
35. Can you think of an example of a conflict we had that you feel we dealt with successfully?
36. What would be unacceptable to you in a disagreement?

Relationships and Commitment

Marriage is obviously a long-term commitment, so questions about this topic ensure both partners are comfortable and feel safe in their relationship. Every partner has certain expectations, and depending on the situation, these questions can help you both better understand the needs of the other.

37. What was a time when you felt most connected and loved in our relationship?
38. How can we make a conscious decision to tell each other if we feel we're being taken for granted?
39. What does our commitment mean to you?
40. What is the most romantic thing we have done together, and why?
41. Why do you want to be married, and why do you want to be married to me?
42. What are the three things you most appreciate about me?

43. What are the three things you most admire about me?
44. What first attracted you to me?
45. How do you envision your life in five years? In 10? In 20?
46. What is your definition of infidelity?
47. What do you love about me that you hope never changes?
48. What do you think you will have to give up when we get married or move in together?
49. Is there anything you would like me to change or give up after we get married?
50. What kind of partner do you aspire to be?
51. Do you need to have some time alone and if so, how often?
52. Are you willing to schedule one evening a week to regularly sit down with each other and catch up about deep stuff?
53. What support do you expect from me in hard times (illness, death, unemployment), and what does that support look like?

Finances and Money

In most marriages, financial issues are one of the leading causes of divorce. This topic can be uncomfortable and stressful, but making sure you have a similar financial plan will save you time and conflict. Answering these difficult questions honestly will give you more clarity about your expectations.

54. How much money do you make?
55. How much debt do you have (student loans, credit card, mortgage), if any?

56. How comfortable are you borrowing money?
57. What was your family's attitude toward money, and how do they resemble yours?
58. Are you more a saver or a spender?
59. Are we going to make it a priority to save money together?
60. Do we sign a prenuptial agreement before we get married?
61. Do you agree to consult with me any significant expense ahead of time, even if you are planning to use your own money?
62. Are you comfortable creating a budget for our married life together?
63. How are we going to share the expenses after we get married?
64. Are we going to have a joint bank account?
65. If you have an ex or children from previous marriages, what are your financial obligations to them?
66. Do you have any other financial obligations to another person, whether for legal or moral reasons, that I should know about?
67. What is important to you financially — owning a house, a nice car, expensive clothing, traveling?
68. What is more important for you, the size of a house or its location?
69. Do you plan to buy or rent?
70. How important is contributing to charity to you, and which charities are your favorites?
71. Who's going to pay the bills?

Communication

Couples who don't openly communicate run into problems, causing a disconnect and feelings of carelessness. Understanding how your partner handles their emotions is a good indicator of how they approach conflict resolution.

72. How comfortable are you with me sharing my feelings, even if they are negative?
73. How do you feel when I disagree with you?
74. Would you tell me a white lie to avoid hurting my feelings?
75. Is there something in the way I say things when I'm angry that makes you feel criticized?
76. Do you think I nag too much?
77. Have I ever disappointed you or caused you pain?
78. Have we talked through those times and resolved them, or are they still affecting our relationship?
79. Is there anything about me that attracts you now but might annoy you over the years?

Work and Career

Before getting married, couples might have an idealized vision of a relationship in which there is always plenty of quality time to be spent together. But in day-to-day life, it's essential for spouses to support each other's careers and professional growth as well. Whether it's a new job or working late, couples need to find the harmonious balance that works for them.

80. If I get offered my dream job in another part of the country, would you be willing to move with me?

81. Would you be OK with me quitting my job to take care of our children?
82. What if I can't stand my work situation, and I just need a break?
83. What are your career goals in both the near and distant future?
84. Would you be understanding if I worked long hours for extended periods of time?

Lifestyle Preferences

To deal with the minutia of daily life, partners should prioritize each other's personal preferences and interests. This can be as simple as making their preferred dinner, or as complicated as doing house chores.

85. What does your ideal day off look like?
86. What does your ideal vacation look like?
87. How do you feel about my single friends? Would you be OK if I partied with them once in a while?
88. What is your attitude toward drugs and drinking?
89. How do you feel about my cleanliness and neatness standards?
90. How will we divide the chores?
91. Are you OK hiring help to clean?
92. Who will do the shopping and cooking in our relationship?
93. How often do you plan to eat out? And what kind of restaurants do you enjoy most?
94. How important is for you to eat at the dinner table, with no TV or electronic distractions?

Faith and Spirituality

It could be that neither of you are religious, or one partner may be more spiritual than the other. This is a particularly essential topic to discuss and respect is the priority here. And when your partner feels respected, it allows your relationship to grow.

95. What are your spiritual or religious beliefs?
96. How important is for you to keep a spiritual or religious practice?
97. How involved are you in your spiritual or religious community?
98. How much do you expect me to be involved in your spiritual or religious activities?
99. Do you expect our children to be raised with a certain spiritual or religious faith and, if so, what would that look like?
100. Do you expect our children to go through certain religious rituals, such as a baptism, bar or bat mitzvah, or first communion?

Lee and Darlene Constant

REFERENCE NOTES

Becoming Mrs. Constant, *Article: 9 Important Communication Skills for Every Relationship by*: Victor *William Harris University of Florida*

Article: Four Different Communication Styles, by: Dr. Norman Wright

Setting Boundaries with the In-Laws *Dr. Henry Cloud and Dr. John Townsend, Boundaries: How to Say Yes, How to Say* No to *Take Control of Your Life*

Before You Say I Do *Article:* 100 Questions you and your Fiancé should discuss in great detail before getting married. You can find this article @ yourtango.com

What's Your Sex Language *Psychologist and author Douglas Weiss PhD, Author of* 5 *Sex Languages*

The Dirty S Word, *The Eight Myths about Submission, MarriageTrac Article by* Nancy DeMoss

About

D.C. CONSTANT

D.C. Constant is the Founder and CEO of The Successful Wives Network, LLC where she leads the organization toward assisting wives in pursuit of enhancing their Personal and Professional Development. With over 20 years in Non-profit, she has a proven track record, in Business Development and Management, Strategic Planning, Workshop Training & Leadership Development.

D.C. is passionate about the health of marriages and believes every wife can be successful in her own right. She's been married 25 years (*yeah, we know she doesn't look it*) to her amazing husband, whom she's still trying to convince to purchase her a Golden Retriever as a playmate to Cooper, their Yorkshire Terrier.

WAIT THERE'S MORE!

BOOK
D.C. CONSTANT

To book D.C. for speaking engagements, coaching, seminars and workshops, please contact:

602.668.9858

www.dcconstant.com

info@darleneconstant.com

JOIN OUR TRIBE!

Stay connected, learn more, and become a part of The Successful Wives Network™

www.thesuccessfulwivesnetwork.com

The Constant Family ~ Lee, Amber-Lee, D.C. and Cooper